THE SOUL OF EDUCATIONAL LEADERSHIP

VOLUME 7

DATA ENHANCED LEADERSHIP

ALAN M. BLANKSTEIN ❧ PAUL D. HOUSTON ❧ ROBERT W. COLE

EDITORS

A JOINT PUBLICATION

American Association of School Administrators

CORWIN PRESS
A SAGE Company
Thousand Oaks, CA 91320

For information:

Corwin
A SAGE Company
2455 Teller Road
Thousand Oaks,
    California 91320
(800) 233-9936
Fax: (800) 417-2466
www.corwinpress.com

SAGE India Pvt. Ltd.
B 1/I 1 Mohan Cooperative
    Industrial Area
Mathura Road,
    New Delhi 110 044
India

SAGE Ltd.
1 Oliver's Yard
55 City Road
London EC1Y 1SP
United Kingdom

SAGE Asia-Pacific Pte. Ltd.
33 Pekin Street #02-01
Far East Square
Singapore 048763

Printed in the United States of America

Library of Congress Cataloging-in-Publication Data

Data-enhanced leadership/Alan M. Blankstein, Paul D. Houston, Robert W. Cole, editors.
    p. cm.—(The soul of educational leadership; v.7)
Includes bibliographical references and index.
ISBN 978-1-4129-4934-7 (pbk.)
    1. Educational leadership. I. Blankstein, Alan M., 1959- II. Houston, Paul D. III. Cole, Robert W. IV. Title.

LB2806.D265 2010
371.20028′5—dc22   2009038918

This book is printed on acid-free paper.

10   11   12   13   14   10   9   8   7   6   5   4   3   2   1

Acquisitions Editor:	Debra Stollenwerk
Associate Editor:	Julie McNall
Production Editor:	Libby Larson
Copy Editor:	Teresa Herlinger
Typesetter:	C&M Digitals (P) Ltd.
Proofreader:	Theresa Kay
Indexer:	Jean Casalegno
Cover Designer:	Michael Dubowe

CONTENTS

ABOUT THE EDITORS

Alan M. Blankstein is founder and president of the HOPE Foundation, a not-for-profit organization whose honorary chair is Nobel Prize winner Archbishop Desmond Tutu. The HOPE Foundation (Harnessing Optimism and Potential through Education) is dedicated to supporting educational leaders over time in creating school cultures where failure is not an option for any student. HOPE sustains student success.

The HOPE Foundation brought W. Edwards Deming and his work to light in educational circles, beginning with the Shaping Chicago's Future conference in 1988. From 1988 to 1992, in a series of Shaping America's Future forums and PBS video conferences, he brought together scores of national and world leaders including Al Shanker; Peter Senge; Mary Futrell; Linda Darling-Hammond; Ed Zigler; and CEOs of GM, Ford, and other corporations to determine how best to bring quality concepts and those of "learning organizations" to bear in educational systems.

The HOPE Foundation provides professional development for thousands of educational leaders annually throughout North America and other parts of the world, including South Africa. HOPE also provides long-term support for school improvement through leadership academies and intensive on-site school change efforts, leading to dramatic increases in student achievement in diverse settings.

A former "high risk" youth, Blankstein began his career in education as a music teacher and has worked within youth-serving organizations for 20 years, including the March of Dimes; Phi Delta Kappa; and the National Educational Service (NES), which he founded in 1987 and directed for 12 years.

He coauthored with Rick DuFour the *Reaching Today's Youth* curriculum, now provided as a course in 16 states, and has contributed writing to *Educational Leadership, The School Administrator, Executive Educator, High School Magazine, Reaching Today's Youth,* and *EQ + IQ = Best Leadership Practices for Caring and Successful Schools.* Blankstein has provided keynote presentations and workshops for virtually every major educational organization. He is author of the best-selling book *Failure Is Not an Option™: Six Principles That Guide Student Achievement in High-Performing Schools,* which has been awarded "Book of the Year" by the National Staff Development Council and was nominated for three other national and international awards.

Blankstein is on the Harvard International Principals Center's advisory board, has served as a board member for the Federation of Families for Children's Mental Health, is a cochair of Indiana University's Neal Marshall Black Culture Center's Community Network, and is advisor to the Faculty and Staff for Student Excellence mentoring program. He is also an advisory board member for the Forum on Race, Equity, and Human Understanding with the Monroe County Schools in Indiana, and has served on the Board of Trustees for the Jewish Child Care Agency (JCCA) at which he was once a youth-in-residence.

Paul D. Houston served as executive director of the American Association of School Administrators (AASA) from 1994 to 2008. He currently serves as president of the Center for Empowered Leadership (CFEL).

Dr. Houston has established himself as one of the leading spokespersons for American education through his extensive speaking engagements, published articles, and regular appearances on national radio and television.

Dr. Houston has coauthored three books: *Exploding the Myths,* with Joe Schneider; *The Board-Savvy Superintendent,* with Doug Eadie; and *The Spiritual Dimension of Leadership,* with Steven Sokolow. He has also authored three books: *Articles of Faith and Hope for Public Education, Outlooks and Perspectives on American Education,* and *No Challenge Left Behind: Transforming America's Schools Through Heart and Soul.*

Dr. Houston served previously as a teacher and building administrator in North Carolina and New Jersey. He has also served as assistant superintendent in Birmingham, Alabama, and as superintendent of schools in Princeton, New Jersey; Tucson, Arizona; and Riverside, California.

Dr. Houston has also served in an adjunct capacity for the University of North Carolina, Harvard University, Brigham Young University, and Princeton University. He has been a consultant and speaker throughout the United States and overseas, and he has published more than 200 articles in professional journals.

Robert W. Cole is proprietor and founder of Edu-Data, a firm specializing in writing, research, and publication services. He was a member of the staff of *Phi Delta Kappan* magazine for 14 years: assistant editor from 1974–1976, managing editor from 1976–1980, and editor-in-chief from 1981–1988. During his tenure as editor-in-chief, the *Kappan* earned more than 40 Distinguished Achievement Awards from the Association of Educational Publishers, three of them for his editorials.

Since leaving the *Kappan,* Cole has served as founding vice president of the Schlechty Center for Leadership in School Reform (CLSR; 1990–1994). At CLSR, he managed district- and community-wide school reform efforts and led the team that created the Kentucky Superintendents' Leadership Institute. He formed the Bluegrass Leadership Network, in which superintendents worked together to use current leadership concepts to solve reform-oriented management and leadership problems.

As senior consultant to the National Reading Styles Institute (1994–2005), Cole served as editor and lead writer of the Power Reading Program. He and a team of writers and illustrators created a series of hundreds of graded short stories, short novels, and comic books from Primer through Grade 10. Those stories were then recorded by Cole and Dr. Marie Carbo; they are being used by schools all across the United States to teach struggling readers.

Cole has served as a Book Development Editor for the Association for Supervision and Curriculum Development (ASCD), for Corwin, and for Writer's Edge Press. He has been president of the Educational Press Association of America and member of the EdPress Board of Directors. He has presented workshops, master classes, and lectures at universities nationwide, including Harvard University, Stanford University, Indiana University, Xavier University, Boise State University, and the University of Southern Maine. He has served as a special consultant to college and university deans in working with faculties on writing for professional publication. Recently, he began serving as managing editor and senior associate with the Center for Empowered Leadership.

ABOUT THE CONTRIBUTORS

Dr. Kay Burke has served as an award-winning classroom teacher, school administrator, and university instructor. For the past 19 years, she has facilitated professional development workshops for teachers and administrators throughout the United States; delivered keynote addresses; and presented at numerous conferences sponsored by the Association for Supervision and Curriculum Development (ASCD), National Staff Development Council (NSDC), the National Association of Elementary School Principals (NAESP), the National Association of Secondary School Principals (NASSP), the National Middle School Association (NMSA), and the International Reading Association (IRA) as well as international conferences throughout Australia and Canada.

Dr. Burke has written or edited 16 books in the areas of standards-based learning, performance assessment, classroom management, mentoring, and portfolios. She is a coauthor of *Foundations of Meaningful Educational Assessment* (Musial, Nieminen, Thomas, & Burke, 2009). Some of her books published by Corwin include *How to Assess Authentic Learning,* 5th ed. (2009); *What to Do With the Kid Who . . . : Developing Cooperation, Self-Discipline, and Responsibility in the Classroom,* 3rd ed. (2008); *The Portfolio Connection: Student Work Linked to Standards,* 3rd ed. (2008); and *Mentoring Guidebook Level 1: Starting the Journey,* 2nd ed. (2002).

Her best-selling book, *From Standards to Rubrics in Six Steps: Tools for Assessing Student Learning, K–8,* was named a 2007 finalist for the Distinguished Achievement Award from the Association of Educational Publishers. Her latest book, *Balanced Assessment: From Formative to Summative,* is scheduled for publication by Solution Tree Press in the fall of 2009.

Eileen Depka has had a variety of experiences as an educator. Beginning her career as an elementary teacher, she extended her certification to spend years teaching middle school students. Her background also includes work with English language learners and at-risk students.

Depka currently is a district Assistant Superintendent. Her efforts include working with classroom teachers and administrators at all levels in all subjects. Some aspects of her role include dealing with all levels of assessment, analysis of data, as well as promotion of and support during the continuous school improvement process.

Depka presents workshops at the local, regional, and national level on such topics as assessment, data collection and analysis, continuous school improvement, best practices, and differentiation.

She is the author of *Designing Rubrics for Mathematics, Designing Assessment for Mathematics,* and *The Data Guidebook for Teachers and Leaders: Tools for Continuous Improvement,* available through Corwin. Depka has worked as content advisor on educational videos and written online courses. As an instructor at the graduate level, she has taught courses in assessment, the backward design process, and grading for learning.

Eileen is passionate about the belief that all students can achieve at high levels of proficiency and is dedicated to working with educators in their quest to inspire all students to experience academic success.

Dr. Lorna M. Earl is a director of Aporia Consulting Ltd. and a retired Associate Professor from the Department of Theory and Policy Studies at the Ontario Institute for Studies in Education of the University of Toronto. She was the first Director of Assessment for the Ontario Education Quality and Accountability Office, and she has been a researcher and research director in school districts for over 20 years. Dr. Earl holds a doctorate in Epidemiology and Biostatistics, as well as degrees in education and psychology.

Throughout her career, Dr. Earl has concentrated her efforts on policy and program evaluations as a vehicle to enhance learning for pupils and for organizations. She has done extensive work in the areas of literacy and the middle years but has focused on issues related to evaluation of reform and assessment (large-scale and classroom) in many venues around the world. She has worked extensively in schools and with school boards, and has been involved in consultation, research, and staff development with teachers' organizations, ministries of education, school districts, and charitable foundations.

During his 50-year career, **Dr. Roy Forbes** has served as the director of a rural education center, director of an urban education center, director of the National Assessment of Educational Progress, advisor to a governor, and the founding director of SERVE (the Southeast's regional education research and development laboratory). Since his retirement in 1997, he has remained active as a consultant. Currently he is serving part-time as the interim director of the Evaluation Center, College of Education, University of West Georgia.

Peter W. Hill is an educational consultant and advisor. He has held numerous senior positions in school administration and educational research in Australia, the United States, and Hong Kong, including as Chief General Manager of the Department of School Education in Victoria, Australia; as Professor of Leadership and Management at The University of Melbourne; as Director of Research and Development at the National Center on Education and the Economy in Washington, D.C.; and as Secretary General of the Hong Kong Examinations and Assessment Authority. He is coauthor with Michael Fullan and Carmel Crévola of *Breakthrough,* published by Corwin.

Dr. Steven Katz is a director with the research and evaluation firm Aporia Consulting Ltd. and a permanent faculty member in Human Development and Applied Psychology at the Ontario Institute for Studies in Education of the University of Toronto. He is an associate member of the School of Graduate Studies and is the coordinator of the Psychology of Learning and Development initial teacher education strand.

Dr. Katz has a doctorate in human development and applied psychology, with a specialization in applied cognitive science. His areas of expertise include cognition and learning; teacher education; networked learning communities; and the design of data-driven systems for organizational accountability, planning, and improvement. He has received the Governor General's Medal for excellence in his field and has been involved in research and evaluation, professional development, and consulting with a host of educational organizations around the world.

Dr. Douglas Otto, superintendent of the Plano Independent School District, is widely acknowledged as one of the nation's leaders in educational technology, school administration, and school finance. He has led the Plano Independent School District, which serves 54,000 students, since 1995, overseeing its rapid growth in enrollment in a challenging school finance system. He serves as the president of the Texas Schools Finance Coalition and has also served on school finance reform panels in Indiana and Minnesota.

The American Association for School Administrators recognized his accomplishments with its Leadership for Learning Award in 2000 for the total integration of technology into the elementary curriculum. He was named by *eSchool News* as one of the 12 Tech-Savvy Superintendents from across the nation and was also selected as the Region 10 Service Center's nominee for Texas Superintendent of the Year in 2001. He was inducted into the Illinois State University College of Education Hall of Fame in 2002. Committed to the notion that college readiness is a result of thoughtful and conscious preparations, not chance or privilege, Dr. Otto launched the *UR—"University Ready"* Web site in the summer of 2007 to assist students and parents as they prepare for all aspects of the post-secondary experience. In addition, in the spring of 2008, he introduced a family services division within the district as an outreach to the greater community. This initiative incorporates family services, adult literacy, and parent education to enhance support of student achievement.

In 2007, the Plano Independent School District Board of Trustees honored Dr. Otto as the namesake of the future Douglas W. Otto Middle School in honor of his service to school children.

Jesse Rodriguez has had significant management and consulting responsibilities in K–12 U.S. and international education. In 1988, he was charged with managing all administrative and instructional education information systems as well as planning the eventual decentralization of these systems for the Tucson Unified School District, one of the 50 largest school districts in the United States.

At the end of 1999, he resigned his position with the Tucson Public Schools to work full-time as an educational technology consultant. Rodriquez has been a keynote speaker on educational technology issues for numerous organizations including the American Association of School Administrators (AASA), the Association of Educational Service Agencies (AESA), the Association of School Business Officials (ASBO), Compaq, HP, and Microsoft.

INTRODUCTION

ROBERT W. COLE

Credit Paul Houston with the topic of this volume, *Data-Enhanced Leadership*. During the planning phase of this long-running series, Paul, one of the three editors (as well as the recently retired executive director of the American Association of School Administrators, and now president of the Center for Empowered Leadership) made the point that data have enormous power to improve the quality of decisions, but *leaders* are the ones who drive decision making in schools. Data are tools for leaders.

That point of view aligns perfectly with the intent of this entire series, *The Soul of Educational Leadership*. We three editors—Paul Houston, Alan Blankstein, and I—have from the beginning conceived of this undertaking as a toolbox for enriching and sustaining the work of leaders in education. The opening volumes dwelt on some of the larger themes that leaders must attend to. Volume 1, *Engaging Every Learner,* sounded the vitally important note that every student matters deeply, to all of us in and around schools and in our society. Volume 2, *Out-of-the-Box Leadership,* called for transformative leadership, which can come only by thinking differently about the problems and challenges we face.

Succeeding volumes began delving into issues that all leaders must face sooner or later, regardless of their level and type of practice. Volumes 3 and 5, *Sustaining Learning Communities* and

Building Sustainable Leadership Capacity, were closely related, acknowledging in their duality the daunting challenge of creating learning communities that have the power to support enduring change. Volume 3 addressed the difficult task of holding on to, and improving upon, valuable work once it has begun. Volume 5 recognized that developing leadership capacity that is to last requires a clarity of shared moral vision and urgency, leadership in community, and a recognition of the challenges posed by young people's lives outside of school.

Volumes 4 and 6 featured two larger roles of education leaders that are often obscured by the everyday demands that clamor for any leader's attention. In Volume 6, *Leaders as Communicators and Diplomats,* a bevy of superintendents and national leaders wrote with hard-earned understanding of the role of leaders as storytellers, persuaders, conveners, and reframers—people who are skilled at uniting disparate followers in common cause. And Volume 4, *Spirituality in Educational Leadership,* went straight to the heart of the whole enterprise of leadership, acknowledging, as Paul Houston put it, that "the work we do is really more of a calling and a mission than it is a job."

Paul also observed in Volume 4 that "These jobs of ours as educational leaders are difficult and draining. They sap our physical and moral energy. We have to find ways of replenishing the supply." The important work of replenishing our supply is an overriding purpose of this series. From the beginning, we have aimed to provide contributions from leading thinkers and practitioners on the soul-work of educational leadership.

Now comes Volume 7 on the nitty-gritty of using data, rather than allowing data to use you. This volume is akin to lifting the hood of your car to gain a more complete understanding of how it runs, and how it can be fine-tuned to run even better. Paul Houston, leading off with "Using What You Know to Be a More Effective Leader," aptly reminds leaders that "your work with children is more than simply checking the test scores." Not one to overlook the crucial importance of good data to leaders, however, he continues: "Letting *anything* that is mechanical and narrow drive your leadership is a mistake. However, it would be the height of stupidity not to use every tool available to you; the availability of data and the insights it can offer will make you a better leader—it should *enhance* your leadership."

"Educational institutions are awash with data, and much of it is not used well," lament Lorna M. Earl and Steven Katz of Aporia Consulting in "Creating a Culture of Inquiry: Harnessing Data for Professional Learning." Earl, a researcher and research director in school districts for over 20 years, was the first director of assessment for the Ontario Education Quality and Accountability Office; Katz is a permanent faculty member in Human Development and Applied Psychology at the Ontario Institute for Studies in Education (OISE) of the University of Toronto. Earl and Katz encourage the cultivation of "an inquiry habit of mind," calling data "tools that teachers and educational leaders can use to focus and challenge their thinking in ways that result in the creation and sharing of new knowledge."

In "Using Assessment Data to Lead Teaching and Learning," Peter W. Hill affirms that "The future lies in adopting a tri-level approach to data use that explicitly recognizes the different data needs of the system, school leaders, and classroom teachers, and places a much greater emphasis at all levels on formative uses of assessment data." A consultant and advisor who works in the United States, Australia, and Hong Kong, he warns leaders, "The trick lies in getting the right balance at each level and ensuring the alignment of purposes and processes."

An assistant superintendent in Waukesha, Wisconsin, Eileen Depka calls for a systemwide focus on continuous improvement, with data as its foundation, as the key to institutionalizing a data-based decision-making system that will have the power to guide districts to increased success. In "Data: Institutionalizing the Use of a Four-Letter Word," she concludes that "connecting the dots between data reviews and continuous improvement planning provides a clear guiding purpose for the consistent use of data."

"Too many educators seem to rely on the data generated from high-stakes standardized tests," warns Kay Burke in "Using Data to Drive Instruction and Assessment in the Standards-Based Classroom." Burke, an award-winning teacher, school administrator, university instructor, and author, has written or edited 16 books on standards-based learning, performance assessment, classroom management, mentoring, and portfolios. She observes that "the data provided by formative and summative classroom assessments is even more valuable" to the intertwined processes of instruction and assessment.

Douglas Otto, superintendent of the Plano (Texas) Independent School District, describes his district's journey toward the more efficient use of data. In "Data: One District's Journey," he observes that the real challenge in data-enhanced decision making is "getting the right data, to the right person, at the right time, in the right format." In this process, he emphasizes, "the questions regarding what kinds of data are needed" are just as important as the databases themselves.

If getting the right data into the right hands is important, it would not be possible without the use of technology. In "Information and Communications Technology in Education," Jesse Rodriguez emphasizes the importance of technology for collecting and analyzing data and assisting in accomplishing the stated goals of school systems. Rodriguez also explains how the relationship between the district superintendent and the chief information officer (CIO) of a school district is central to the district's effectiveness in implementing and using technology. In the 20 years since he managed all administrative and instructional education information systems for the Tucson Unified School District, Rodriguez has worked extensively in these areas all around the world. "One-to-one computing, regardless of the technology used, is a desired, and desirable, outcome," he writes; the key is "implementing an information network capable of supporting this outcome."

During his 50-year career, Roy Forbes has served as the director of both a rural and an urban education center, director of the National Assessment of Educational Progress (NAEP), advisor to a governor, and the founding director of SERVE (the Southeast's regional education research and development laboratory). He remains active as a consultant and currently serves as part-time interim director of the Evaluation Center, College of Education, University of West Georgia. In "Some Pitfalls in the Use of Data—and How to Avoid Them," Forbes provides commonsense guidelines to the use of data. The moral he provides is this: "Data is your friend. It exists to assist you in making decisions. But approach it carefully! If not, it may turn around and bite you."

As Alan Blankstein wrote in the first chapter of the first volume in this series, this work of education "is not easy or simple work, yet it can be done." And the data with which we are armed—especially the data we have amassed that allow us to know what has worked most successfully to help teachers and students—assist us in that work. All along, that has been the guiding purpose of this series: to arm and strengthen you for the challenges you face.

CHAPTER ONE

USING WHAT YOU KNOW TO BE A MORE EFFECTIVE LEADER

PAUL D. HOUSTON

In his autobiography, *Disturbing the Universe,* the physicist Freeman Dyson (2001) relates that he was profoundly affected by a book he read in his childhood called *The Magic City,* by Edith Nesbit (1910). While Nesbit's book is a story about a crazy universe, Dyson came to understand that the universe she described bore a remarkable resemblance to the one we live in. One of the laws of life in the magic city is that if you wish for something, you can have it. If it is a machine, however, you are compelled to keep it and live with it the rest of your life.

Dyson used this metaphor to help us understand what humankind had brought about with the advent of nuclear energy. As we have moved deeper into the Information Age, ruled by ever-smaller yet increasingly powerful computers, we have created quite a box for ourselves out of those wonderful little boxes. Now—for better and maybe for worse—we must coexist with these machines. As much as we control them, they also control us.

In his book *Management of the Absurd,* Richard Farson (1997) posits a number of paradoxes that leaders must consider. One of those is this: "Technology creates the opposite of its intended purpose" (p. 44). Farson suggests that every time technology is created to make things easier, it simultaneously makes things harder.

The yin and yang created by the possibilities and perils of technology have bedeviled school leaders for decades.

If nothing else, the yin and yang created by the possibilities and perils of technology have bedeviled school leaders for decades. It seems to me that Farson and Dyson have laid out the situation quite clearly for us. We have created something amazing and wonderful—but we have to live with all its implications. The challenge for school leaders is to find a way to make the best of this dilemma.

I was a young superintendent when computers were first being introduced into schools. It is hilarious to look back 30 years and think of how we viewed this new "gift" at the time. Our first thought was that we needed to teach kids how to program, so they could grow up and be computer programmers. That quickly shifted to the notion that we could use computers to teach skills—and computer-assisted instruction burst onto the scene. Children were sent off to computer labs to sit in front of a screen and respond to prompts made by these wonderful new machines. This was going to solve all our achievement problems.

As a superintendent, I knew a couple of things. The first was that I couldn't possibly ignore computers. To do so would mark me as a leader who was behind the times. I would be handicapping my students—sending them into a new world, but without the tools to make the most of it. The second thing I learned was that technology is expensive. So I was caught in one of those paradoxes: I had to have computers, but I had to justify their expense. But wouldn't it be wonderful if these new machines actually had the power to transform education?

I was lucky. At that time, I was superintendent in Princeton, New Jersey. It was a community that had solid resources, was forward-thinking, and (perhaps most important) saw its children as the next generation of "masters of the universe." This somewhat arrogant mind-set allowed us to think about technology differently. We couldn't imagine that we were merely creating the next generation of programmers or that our children could sit for hours in front of a nonhuman screen, merely responding to its orders and commands. Our children were the ones who needed to be doing the commanding!

Therefore, as I said, we approached this new technology in a different way. We decided to view it as a tool to be wielded by our students rather than a force to be followed. So we *did* teach programming, but only as a means of creating programs that would give the students the ability to control the technology. We taught kindergartners how to do simple programming of robots using the LOGO programming language, and taught high school kids how to do more advanced programming. We put computers in English classes and made sure all the kids could type so that they could do word processing. We worked with the *Wall Street Journal* (which was produced just outside of Princeton) to develop a very early version of online research that allowed students to step up their ability to write papers and do projects.

Of course, we discovered some of the dark side of the gift we had been given. We realized that "garbage in" really did create "garbage out." If students didn't use their language skills with some precision, they received all kinds of useless information on their searches. And we realized pretty quickly that this new way of doing research was also a much more efficient way to cheat, and that it was harder for teachers to know whether something was truly outstanding or just a great job of plagiarism.

But we worked through these and other issues and kept ahead of the curve by buying more computers, and newer models as they came out. Of course, we also realized that technology was a black hole of expenditures for the system, and we were still faced with the nagging question, is it worth it?

To this day, computer companies and school leaders are plagued by the need to justify the "value added" of these expensive machines. And even as the costs came down, the need to buy more machines, to create "take home" programs, and to expand the possibilities offered causes a push for more and more computers—and therefore ever-greater expenditures. Along the way, we have realized that the computers wouldn't fix themselves, so departments have had to be created to stay on top of that issue as well. And *then* we realized that of the many different kinds of computers out there, each had to be repaired a different way, so the dilemma of choice and flexibility versus standardization came into play.

—————— ✿ ——————

As typewriters were replaced by desktop computers, and mainframes replaced by distributed networks, operations became more efficient—and increasingly dependent on technology. If the system was down, no one could work.

Meanwhile, at the back-office level there was a growing realization that these wonderful new contraptions could be used to keep the books and inventories, sort out personnel records, keep track of attendance and test scores, and generally make the business side of the education operation more efficient—until there was a breakdown, that is. I have seen district offices brought to their knees by "glitches" in the system. As typewriters were replaced by desktop computers, and mainframes replaced by distributed networks, operations became more efficient—and increasingly dependent on technology. If the system was down, no one could work.

Here is truly the curse that Dyson and Farson wrote about: Once you wish for it and you have it, you are stuck with it. And while it makes one part of your work easier, it makes others more difficult.

As American education moved boldly into the era of accountability, leaders began to recognize that technology could help here also—by providing faster and more comprehensive feedback on how they might understand the available data and use it effectively to enhance student achievement.

Now I have to throw in a few caveats here. Accountability is more than test scores. When the public says it wants accountability, it means accountability across a wide spectrum. It wants accountability in compensation. The economic meltdown of the fall of 2008 proved at least one thing—people who make billion-dollar screwups should not get million-dollar bonuses. Main Street understood that long before Wall Street figured it out. The public wants to know how its money is spent. That calls for clear and transparent budgets. Even the *language* used by educators must be considered. It is hard to be accountable if you speak a language that the public cannot comprehend. Educators are often accused of using "educationese" to sound like they know something, when simple language would be much more persuasive. So accountability is more than student achievement.

Likewise, however, student achievement is more than test scores. I have been a vocal critic of No Child Left Behind (NCLB), that titanic federal attempt to raise student achievement. I was concerned about it, not because I oppose raising student achievement and would like to see children left behind, but because NCLB was an overly simplistic approach to a pretty complex process.

Just because most of us have learned to read doesn't mean that learning to read is the same as learning to ride a bicycle. Reading involves a pretty amazing set of skills and insights that must be put together in just the right way for success to ensue. Likewise, being an educated person means more than simply mastering basic skills. My guess is that the folks who drove the economy into the ground, or those who committed massive fraud (Bernie Madoff comes quickly to mind), probably had pretty good scores on their achievement tests. But they were clearly missing some important components in their education. It proves once again the wisdom attributed to Albert Einstein, who observed that "not everything that can be counted counts and not everything that counts can be counted."

Having said all that, in education we are currently in a mode that places major emphasis on those things that can be measured. Unfortunately, right now the state of the art in assessment means that simple, low-cost tests (which are the ones used because they are the most affordable) are also the least satisfactory form of assessment. Moreover, when you emphasize only those things that can be measured, you can leave out some very important factors.

Therefore, the first lesson I would offer to school leaders today is to know, deep down, that your work with children is more than simply checking the test scores. I do *not* mean that you shouldn't be using the data you do have—making use of all the tools available is critical for any leader. But you have to know what you know, and then use it properly.

The title of this volume is *Data-Enhanced Leadership*. The term *enhanced* was chosen deliberately. Dozens of volumes have been written that use the notion of "data-*driven* decision making." There are problems with that idea. Letting *anything* that is mechanical and narrow drive your leadership is a mistake. However, it would be the height of stupidity not to use every tool available to you; the availability of data and the insights it can offer will make you a better leader—they should *enhance* your leadership.

When I went to Tucson as superintendent, I wanted to raise student achievement. A big part of that had to be raising test scores. This was before NCLB, so the weight of the federal government wasn't hanging over me, but community dissatisfaction with how the kids were learning definitely affected my planning. So I worked with my technology wizard, Jesse Rodriguez (who contributes an extremely practical chapter to this book). While I started by trying to push Jesse to give me a better system of measuring and weighing outcomes, the conversation quickly turned into Jesse's pushing *me* to be clear on what I wanted. He said, essentially, "Look, I can give you data in lots of different forms. But what are you trying to do? What do you want at the end of the day?"

Those were fair questions—and ones that I'm afraid too few leaders answer for themselves. My back-and-forth discussions with Jesse produced a program that focused on the bottom fourth of our students. These were the ones who were clearly lacking the skills to be successful, and the ones we would be losing before graduation. If we could raise their learning, it would lift the whole system. So I wanted to know how each classroom was doing in each school, and I wanted to know how each teacher was doing.

Let me add a sidelight here: I believe all the current talk of "merit pay" based on student performance is probably overblown. Each year, a teacher faces a different roomful of children with different needs. It is hard (and probably not smart) to use year-to-year comparisons on test scores to decide income. Too much can go wrong.

For example, what happens if one year, by chance, the teacher has a classful of high-flyers and the next year, a class where few can get off the ground? Is the comparison of test scores fair? And we know from the authors of *Freakonomics* (Levitt & Dubner, 2005) that if teacher pay is tied to a single score, it creates a perverse incentive to cheat. One must be cautious in using student tests to determine teacher pay. However, if you have data running over several years that take into consideration children's level coming into the class, and teacher X consistently underperforms with his students compared to teachers Y and Z, then at least you have a starting point in looking at evaluation as a means to improve him or to rid the system of him.

Well, Jesse ended up building a system that gave me exactly the data I had asked for. His system offered a tool to the principals and central office staff that allowed them to work on those areas that needed improvement within the school as well as look at teacher performance.

We also did something in the mid-1980s that is currently a topic of national debate: We looked for *growth*. We ranked our schools, not by their scores, but by their growth in student achievement. This gave recognition and hope to faculties that were working in some of the most difficult schools. They were doing more with their children than was happening in some of our more affluent areas. We did have to factor in the "topping-off effect." That is, it is harder to grow if you are already at the 90th percentile than if you are in the bottom 10 percent. However, since we focused on the bottom quartile of students—and every school had a bottom quartile—it smoothed out the differences between schools. Data became a source of conversation among administrators, and it also allowed us to focus more on problem areas.

> *The first commandment in data-enhanced leadership is to know what you are trying to do. What outcomes are most important to you and your district? What form do they need to be in to help people move forward?*

This is just one story of using data to enhance a leader's decision making. There are many, many more ways to do it. The current context of accountability dictates that leaders focus on outcomes. But simply reporting outcomes or exhorting staff to do better (and excoriating them when they fail) will not work. *Leadership is not just showing people where they need to go—it is showing them how to get there.* Creating and using a system that allows available information to be shaped into meaningful patterns for staff and community so that improvement can take place is at the heart of the leader's role today. Enhancing decision making is also enhancing the quality of life for students and staff.

There are a few more things that leaders must consider. In moving the system toward using technology and its fruits, you have to lead by example. I know leaders who still do not use the Internet, and who have their secretaries print out all their emails because they don't use the technology in the office. Staff members need to see you using technology as a tool in your office if you hope to require them to use it for improving student learning.

As I said earlier, I was an early user, placing a computer on my desk in 1980 and using it as a tool. I will quickly admit, though, that as the pace of technology has advanced, my own use of it has not advanced at the same rate. But computers have become a tool I can't live without.

If you want to know how your students are doing or how your teachers are performing, you must be a user of the available technology. Moreover, you must lead by example. When I was superintendent in Tucson, I wanted my staff to begin using email. Many of them simply would not give it a try, so I devised a simple solution: I began using email to communicate with them. After that, when a meeting was held that they "didn't know about" or an issue was discussed that seemed new to them, I would simply point out that they had received an email about it from me. Soon they were all using email.

The second thing you have to do as a leader is develop a good working relationship with your chief information officer (CIO). (Well, actually you first need to make sure you have one.) Even in smaller districts, someone should be tasked with this role, and then given support, visibility, and authority. Two of the most important staff members on any district staff today are the CIO and the public relations (PR) person. The CIO can gather and form the data available to make them useful and meaningful, and the PR person can help you get these valuable data out, in understandable form, to the community. That is real accountability, and it's also using data to inform decisions and to inform the public.

Finally, as I indicated above, the first commandment in data-enhanced leadership is to know what you are trying to do. What outcomes are most important to you and your district? What form do they need to be in to help people move forward? One of the most important qualities of leadership is clarity—being clear on what is expected and what is happening. This leads to transparency and to positive action.

Yes, Dyson and Farson were correct. When you wish for a tool and you get it, you have to live with it. Technology is here to stay. The use of data is central to the role of leader in today's context. You have to live with that and turn the dilemmas that come with it into positive action. Leadership is about using what you have to get what you want and what the organization needs.

References

Dyson, F. (2001). *Disturbing the universe.* New York: Basic Books.
Farson, R. (1997). *Management of the absurd.* New York: Free Press.
Levitt, S. D., & Dubner, S. J. (2005). *Freakonomics.* London: Allen Lane.
Nesbit, E. (1910). *The magic city.* London: Macmillan.

CHAPTER TWO

CREATING A CULTURE OF INQUIRY

Harnessing Data for Professional Learning

LORNA M. EARL AND STEVEN KATZ

In *Leading Schools in a Data-Rich World: Harnessing Data for School Improvement* (Earl & Katz, 2006), we highlighted the use of data for informed decision making and insisted that data must be used to serve continuous inquiry, not just to answer the question of the day. We are certainly advocates of using data, but we are also concerned about data becoming a diversion rather than an aid to wise decisions. As we wrote in that book,

> We believe that real benefits accrue from "getting to know" data as part of an ongoing process of educational change and using it locally to investigate real issues in particular schools, as a way of deciding what to do next. We are concerned that schools are being pushed and enslaved by data rather than being steered by leaders, with data providing information that they can use to engage in thoughtful planning and make reasoned and targeted decisions to move towards continuous improvement. (p. ix)

Educational institutions are awash with data, and much of it is not used well (Earl & Katz, 2006; Stoll, Fink, & Earl, 2003). As Hess (2008) reminds us, we have come from a time when educational leaders dismissed data and systematic research as having limited utility to a time when every education conference and magazine is rife with data-based decision making and research-based practice. He also warns about using data:

> I fear that data-based decision making and research-based practice can stand in for careful thought, serve as dressed-up rationales for the same old fads, or be used to justify incoherent proposals. Because few educators are inclined to denounce data, there has been an unfortunate tendency to embrace glib new solutions rather than ask the simple question: What exactly does it mean to use data or research to inform decisions?
>
> Today's enthusiastic embrace of data has waltzed us directly from a petulant resistance to performance measures to a reflexive and unsophisticated reliance on a few simple metrics. (p. 12)

Like Hess, we believe that data add to institutional decision making but that using data means much more than the simplistic application of "half-baked" ideas in the name of evidence-based decision making. Data alone do not answer questions; instead, they provide decision makers with additional information to think with as they consider complex educational issues from a range of vantage points. Data are tools to be used by leaders in a complex process of understanding issues better, considering nuance and context, and focusing and targeting their work productively. This is a *human* activity that requires not only capturing and organizing ideas but also turning information into meaningful actions (Earl & Katz, 2006). Used thoughtfully, data are dynamic levers for improving schools and schooling, but there is always the risk that hubris, faddism, or untamed enthusiasm will distort and reduce data's potential power (Hess, 2008).

Data alone do not answer questions; instead, they provide decision makers with additional information to think with as they consider complex educational issues from a range of vantage points.

USING DATA FOR SCHOOL IMPROVEMENT

The last 25 years have shown us that changing schools in any large-scale and sustainable way is a difficult and complex process (Elmore, 1996). Jurisdictions around the world are struggling to find strategies and processes that will result in enhanced learning for students and receive widespread support in the educational community and beyond. There are no "quick fixes." School leaders are faced with the daunting task of anticipating the future and making conscious adaptations to their practices, in order to keep up with and respond to an ever-changing environment. If schools are to succeed in a rapidly changing and increasingly complex world, it is vital that they grow, develop, adapt, and take charge of change so that they can control their own futures (Stoll et al., 2003). Schools that are able to take charge of change, rather than being controlled by it, have been shown to be more effective and to improve more rapidly than schools that are not able to do so (Gray, Hopkins, Reynolds, Wilcox, Farrell, & Jesson, 1999; Stoll & Fink, 1996).

Like many other leaders, leaders in the field of education are discovering that they need to go beyond their tacit knowledge and intuition. There is not enough time for adaptation by trial and error or for experimentation with fads that inevitably lose their appeal. In today's "knowledge society," evidence, data, and information have become critical elements in decision making. At the same time, there is an increasing awareness that the hard work of educational change takes place in the hearts and minds of the people who live and work in schools. Just having data is not enough.

Leaders who use data well believe that schools can make a difference; their model of educational change is focused on changing schools to ensure better services and better learning for all students. They hold a view of school improvement like the one described by Louise Stoll (2004): "'Real' school improvement comes from within and is about the ongoing and sustainable learning of students and all those inside and outside schools who care about pupil learning" (p. 4). It is important to note that this definition highlights student learning but also includes learning for the adults who work in schools. It suggest that educators, individually and collectively, routinely learn from the world around them and apply this learning to new situations so that they can continue on a path toward their goals in an ever-changing context (Stoll & Earl, 2003).

Michael Barber (2002), a national policy advisor on education in England, uses the chart in Figure 2.1 to describe trends in educational reform over the past 40 years as a function of the knowledge base on which it has been founded and the locus of responsibility and decision making.

Barber (2002) portrays the 1970s as a time of "uninformed professional judgment," in which educators operated largely as individuals within broad policy guidelines and relied on their personal professional perspectives to make decisions. This was the era of "leave us alone to teach." The 1980s were a time of "uninformed prescription"; governments took direct control of education and dictated prescriptive directions, often without appealing to any knowledge base other than their own ideological views. National or federal programs proliferated, with centrally directed curriculum and assessment systems. In the 1990s, governments still controlled the educational agenda, but they began to draw on research and other evidence to inform their policies. Barber sees the 2000s as an era of "informed professional judgment," in which control of education ought to be returned to educators, but now with the explicit requirement that they act as informed professionals. And that means using evidence and research to justify and support educational decisions.

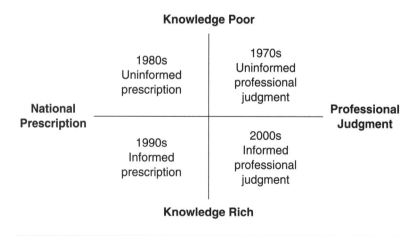

Figure 2.1

IT'S ABOUT LEARNING—PROFESSIONAL LEARNING

Our conception of using data in the service of wise decision making is grounded in a conviction that improved learning outcomes for students is the ultimate goal of decision making, and that more and better learning for students depends on informed professional judgment that results in changes in classrooms and schools. To bring about these two outcomes successfully will require new learning for both teachers and leaders.

Figure 2.2 provides a generalized model of the core elements necessary for school improvement. Although many influences and processes can encourage school improvement, professional learning is the heart of any school-based activity that will result in deeper learning and success for students.

This model is conceptually simple but operationally complex. As Fullan (2006) states, the core of improving schools rests with professionals continuously improving learning and progress at all levels so that their collective efficacy enables them to "raise the bar and close the gap of student learning for all students" (p. 28). It is increasingly clear that deep and productive professional learning is critical to educational change.

Our position about the manner in which data shape practice in productive ways has been reinforced by work done within the Best Evidence Synthesis Programme of the New Zealand Ministry of Education (for more information about this program, see www .educationcounts.govt.nz/themes/BES). One of these Best Evidence Syntheses, on Professional Learning and Development, examines studies in professional learning that have had demonstrated impact

Figure 2.2   Professional Learning at the Core

on student learning (Timperley, Wilson, Barrar, & Fung, 2008). This review provides a backdrop for thinking about how teachers and leaders can use data to identify what they need to know, make informed decisions about changes to practice, build their capacity, and check on the success of their ventures over time.

Timperley et al. (2008) found that people cannot adapt descriptions of effective practice to their own contexts unless they first understand the theoretical principles that explain why the practices are effective. Professional learning that contributed to student learning was deeply grounded in the reality of the teachers' own classrooms and was linked to new learning for the teachers, with both practical and theoretical explanations about the ways in which they could change their practices to better serve their students.

Timperley et al. (2008) encapsulated this work in a powerful inquiry cycle for changing practices to influence student learning (see Figure 2.3). This cycle begins with a consideration of student learning needs. Once a student's learning needs are understood, the teacher moves to an explicit articulation of the relationship between current teaching practice and the student's learning requirements, and then charts a course for professional learning that will both deepen professional knowledge and translate into changes in practice. This process of professional inquiry is cyclical but forward-moving; it gives explicit attention to the new practices for teachers but does not end with one iteration. As practices change and students are better served, teachers move on to a new consideration of student learning needs and proceed through the cycle again. Inquiry and professional learning are inseparable in this model; they merge in a forward-moving, *progressive* way.

Our recent work is consistent with this inquiry cycle. We have found that collaborative inquiry is one of the most powerful enablers of changes in practice that can influence student learning (Earl & Katz, 2007). This process merges deep collaboration (in the form of rigorous and challenging joint work) with inquiry, and is consistent with Little's (2005) reference to a large body of research suggesting that conditions for improving learning and teaching are strengthened when teachers collectively consider evidence about the current state of affairs, question ineffective teaching routines, examine new conceptions of teaching and learning, find generative means to acknowledge and respond to difference and conflict, and engage actively in supporting one another's professional growth. By reviewing their

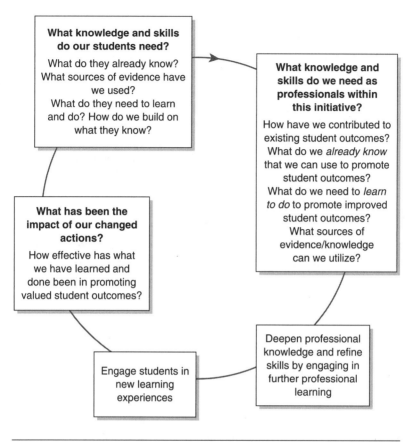

Figure 2.3   Professional Learning Inquiry Cycle

SOURCE: Timperley, Wilson, Barrar, & Fung, 2008.

experiences of learning, focusing at each stage on their *purpose, strategy,* the *effects,* their *feelings,* and the *context,* teachers can review their learning, learn about that learning, and apply what they have learned to their future learning.

We have found that collaborative inquiry is one of the most powerful enablers of changes in practice that can influence student learning.

In recent decades, we have learned a great deal about how people learn; the push for scaling up of reforms has begun to focus attention on how *teachers* learn. Putnam and Borko (2002) describe three factors they maintain are involved in facilitating the construction, and reconstruction, of teacher learning. Attending to these factors is necessary if professional development activities are used to facilitate teacher learning in order to change existing practices. First, Putnam and Borko describe the role of "cognition as situated" in constructing professional learning within the physical and social contexts in which an activity takes place. *How a person learns* a particular set of knowledge and skills and *the situation in which a person learns* become a fundamental part of what is learned. The second factor identified by Putnam and Borko is "cognition as social." This factor influences the construction and reconstruction of professional learning because, as they explain, "Interactions with the people in one's environment are major determinants of both what is learned and how learning takes place" (p. 5). The third factor, "cognition as distributed," suggests that learning is distributed among individuals, with many different people holding part of the knowledge. Yet in classrooms and professional development events, we tend to focus on individual learning and expect teachers to operate in isolation from one another.

Putnam and Borko's (2002) work suggests that professional learning is influenced by the context in which the learning takes place as well as the interactions with other individuals in that context. For instance, a change-oriented school could assist staff members in applying their new learning in their individual classrooms through fostering dialogue with others who are engaged in the same activity. Moreover, distributed learning implies a team-oriented approach to individual professional learning as well as the creation of new collective knowledge. Individuals are not learning alone but are sharing or distributing their learning. This collective approach to professional learning is why Putnam and Borko emphasize the importance of "discourse communities" in promoting educational change.

In their 10-year Learning How to Learn project, Mary James and her colleagues in the United Kingdom have found that collaborative inquiry practices emerged as the key influence on teachers' capacity to promote learning autonomy in their students (James & McCormick, in press).

In this chapter, we maintain that deep, sustained changes depend on a particular kind of professional learning that is context-specific, social, and distributed. We believe that collaborative inquiry that challenges existing thinking and practices drives school improvement, because it attends to both shared learning activities as well as individual knowledge formation. If deep change comes from creating new knowledge, then a fundamental challenge for educators and education is to operate in a way that facilitates ongoing knowledge creation and sharing among members of the community, as a means of tapping into and processing both tacit and explicit knowledge. Members of the education community need to function as *knowledge workers* who engage in a productive interchange between tacit and explicit knowledge in order to generate new collective knowledge that can then be codified and made accessible throughout the entire organization (Hakkarainen, Palonen, Paavola, & Lehtinen, 2004). They engage in conscious and intentional efforts to reframe "what they know" as "what they *think* they know," in order to subject these knowledge *hypotheses* to scrutiny and challenge in relation to available evidence.

Hakkarainen et al. (2004) describe a *dynamic spiral,* critical for knowledge creation and sharing, which contains seven elements through which knowledge is converted and moved from individuals to groups and back again. Although the spiral moves through these stages, it is also iterative, with various switchbacks and repeats possible along the way. The seven elements are as follows:

1. *Creating Context.* The starting point for the process of inquiry is an explicit consideration of the extent to which the issues being investigated are worthy of study and personal commitment. This, in essence, creates the context for knowledge creation.

2. *Engaging in Question-Driven Inquiry.* An essential aspect of progressive inquiry is generating one's own problems and questions to guide the inquiry; without questions generated by the participants themselves, there cannot be a genuine process of inquiry. Questions that arise from one's own need to understand have a special value in the process of inquiry.

3. *Generating Working Theories.* Construction of their own working theories guides inquirers to systematically use their background knowledge and become aware of their presuppositions. Progressive inquiry is aimed at the explication of these intuitive ideas.

4. *Critical Evaluation.* Critical evaluation underscores the need to assess the strengths and weaknesses of the tentative

theories (explanations) produced, so as to direct and regulate the evolution of inquiry. It is essential to focus on constructively evaluating the advancement of the inquiry process itself, rather than simply aiming for some predetermined end result.

5. *Searching for New Information.* Searching for and working with "research" is necessary to deepen one's understanding. New information can come from literature, consulting experts, or conducting one's own explorations. Explicit comparison of intuitive working theories with well-established theories makes the limitations of individual and collective knowledge apparent.

6. *Engagement in Deepening Inquiry.* A critical condition for progress is that inquirers focus on improving their ideas by generating more specific questions and searching for new information. The dynamic nature of inquiry is supported by the fact that generating working theories and obtaining new research knowledge makes new guiding questions accessible.

7. *Shared Expertise.* The agent of knowledge creation is not an isolated individual but rather an individual embedded in a community, or even the community itself. All of the preceding aspects of inquiry can be shared with other inquirers. Inquiry can advance substantially through relying on socially distributed cognitive resources and collaborative efforts to enhance shared understanding.

If collaborative inquiry is indeed the engine of teacher learning, then data provide the fuel. Data do not answer questions; instead, they provide lenses for teachers and school leaders to think about and understand their contexts and situations better as a starting point for the kind of professional learning that can change what happens in schools and classrooms. Data are tools that teachers and educational leaders can use to focus and challenge their thinking in ways that result in the creation and sharing of new knowledge, which then has the potential to change their thinking and their practices.

Data are tools that teachers and educational leaders can use to focus and challenge their thinking in ways that result in the creation and sharing of new knowledge.

As fuel for conversation, data can shape the content and provide focus for the discussion. When educators engage in conversations about what evidence means, they can consider the data, generate hypotheses, and establish a range of possible interpretations. Paying attention to data interrupts the status quo and creates the space for multiple alternative views to emerge. This process sets the stage for new knowledge to surface as the participants encounter new ideas or discover that ideas they have held as "truth" fail to hold up under scrutiny. They have the power to use this recognition as an opportunity to rethink what they know and what they do.

LEADERSHIP FOR PROFESSIONAL LEARNING AND STUDENT OUTCOMES

Teaching ranks first in all the school-based factors that can influence student learning in schools, but the actions of leaders have also been linked to improvement in student learning (Leithwood, Louis, Anderson, & Wahlstrom, 2004). Leadership that supports professional learning and student outcomes is not the heroic leadership of an individual; instead, it is the sustained engagement of multiple people around a shared agenda for improvement.

In another New Zealand Best Evidence Synthesis—Leadership for Student Outcomes—Viviane Robinson (2007) identified five dimensions of leadership activities that linked to student outcomes: (1) establishing goals and expectations; (2) strategic resourcing; (3) planning, coordinating, and evaluating teaching and the curriculum; (4) promoting and participating in teacher learning and development; and (5) ensuring an orderly and supportive environment.

Although all five of these dimensions of leadership were related to student outcomes, with effect sizes ranging from .27 to .84, the most powerful one was "promoting and participating in teacher learning and development," with an effect size of .84. This work provides empirical support for school leaders, both formal and informal, to be actively involved with teachers as the lead learners in their school (Robinson, 2007). Linking this leadership activity to the work on collaborative inquiry by Timperley et al. (2008) suggests a clear direction for leaders (again, both formal and informal): *Leaders create the conditions that allow teachers to engage in intensive collaborative inquiry that is contextualized in their work and participate in it with them.* Leaders are themselves learners. They are the facilitators of routine knowledge creation and sharing for themselves and others, as they investigate their own teaching practices and their efforts to improve them.

CREATING THE CONDITIONS FOR EVIDENCE-INFORMED COLLABORATIVE INQUIRY

Although professional learning communities (PLCs) are the "flavor of the day" in educational reform (and there are critiques of problems associated with the way that many such communities have been formed and implemented), professional learning communities offer a powerful venue for the kind of collaborative inquiry that we advocate here. *The trick is to create the conditions for generating new knowledge through a process that merges deep collaboration with evidence and inquiry.* The power of the idea of a PLC is that members of the group engage together in challenges of practice so that their understanding of those challenges grows deeper and is more unified. Through their mutual investigations, proposed solutions emerge that are then tested to see if they help to promote student learning. Through such a repeated process, teaching practice grows more sophisticated and powerful, and the group develops a tighter sense of camaraderie and common purpose. As a result, group members can construct common understanding, share knowledge and experience, and develop common goals (Supovitz, 2006).

As Hakkarainen et al. (2004) describe, knowledge is created through dialogue or conversations that make presuppositions, ideas, beliefs, and feelings explicit and available for exploration. It is in these conversations that new ideas, tools, and practices are created, and during the process the initial knowledge is either substantially enriched or transformed. Innovative solutions arise when people in groups draw on evidence and on outside explicit knowledge and combine it with tacit knowledge in response to authentic problems (Nonaka & Takeuchi, 1995). The engagement with competing theories and the evidence underpinning them requires participants in a conversation to reveal what they believe and why. They must explain their views and why their perspective is preferable to those of others, and also be open to challenge and critique. (And they must be open to *both* "challenge" *and* "critique.") Quite often, personal theories tend to be implicit rather than explicit and assumed rather than tested. Through the process of explaining one's theories to others who hold different views, what is known is made more explicit, along with the values, beliefs, and evidence that underpin them.

Learning how to engage in inquiry as a technique for knowledge creation requires effort; it is hard work to move the natural tendencies of people to want to protect existing understandings and practices. Like any new and complex skill, inquiry takes time and deliberate practice to develop, and all the leaders in a school have a role to play in moving from existing ways of doing business to the spirit of collaborative inquiry.

Instructional leaders have the responsibility for creating opportunities for teachers to get comfortable with *not knowing,* to embrace new learning as a routine part of their work, to participate in the process of examining their own beliefs and practices, and to use data as an entry point for their conversations. This process doesn't begin with the data. Instead, it starts with conversations about what teachers—collectively—want (or need) to know and deciding what data are required to refine their questions. The process is one of thinking and hypothesizing about what forces are at work in relation to the local priorities and context, of talking about what the participants think is going on, and of making their tacit knowledge visible so that they can see what they—both individually and as a group—"believe to be true."

CAPACITIES FOR LEADING IN A DATA-RICH WORLD

Becoming a skilled and confident consumer and user of data for school improvement is not simple or straightforward, nor is it a mechanistic process. It is a skill and an art, a way of thinking and interacting that interrupts (and sometimes *dis*rupts) the status quo. Leaders certainly need to have an understanding of data, but data literacy is only a small part of a process of collaborative inquiry for school improvement. In another publication, we identified what we believe are the key capacities for

Becoming a skilled and confident consumer and user of data for school improvement . . . is a skill and an art, a way of thinking and interacting that interrupts (and sometimes dis*rupts) the status quo.*

leaders in a data-rich world (Earl & Katz, 2006); we believe they still hold true. Leaders for informed professionalism will need to do the following:

- Develop an inquiry habit of mind
- Become data literate
- Create a culture of inquiry in their school community

An Inquiry Habit of Mind

School leaders who use data productively have a mind-set of being in charge of their own destiny, always needing to know more and creating or locating the knowledge that will be useful to them along the way. In this kind of school, leaders are not technicians organizing and manipulating data in prescribed ways, like following a paint-by-number picture; instead, they develop an "inquiry habit of mind"—collecting and interpreting evidence in ways that advance their understanding.

For inquiry to be truly effective, it needs to become a way of doing business, a way of thinking, a *habit of mind,* rather than a discrete event. The definition of a habit is a settled tendency of practice. Habits are things people do both frequently and automatically. Automatically means without conscious attention, and this is especially significant because *automaticity* is an important way in which humans manage their limited cognitive resources. Think about learning to drive, or learning to read. When first learning, your mind was occupied by the mechanics of what you were doing (or trying to do). You thought consciously about moving your foot from the gas pedal to the brake; you thought consciously about the sounds letters made as you worked to decode a word. Few, if any, mental resources were left over to do other things at the same time. In the case of driving, this meant that you couldn't think about what you might like for dinner that night (at least not without increasing your chances of having an accident). In the case of reading, it meant that by the time you had worked out the letter–sound relationships of the words in a sentence, the *meaning* (your comprehension) of the previous sentence was likely lost. Since people learn to read so that they can read to learn, they can't afford to expend valuable cognitive resources on decoding that are needed for comprehension. They need to achieve automaticity in decoding, as a foundation for comprehension. Automaticity is achieved through deliberate practice, and the amount of time spent on deliberate practice is another hallmark characteristic of experts, regardless of the arena. We link *inquiry* to *habit of mind* to emphasize a way of thinking that is a dynamic, iterative system to organize ideas, seek out information, and move closer and closer to understanding some phenomenon. What does this mean for school leaders?

Leaders with an inquiry habit of mind do the following:

- *Value deep understanding.* Leaders with an inquiry habit of mind do not presume an outcome; instead, they allow for a range of outcomes and keep searching for increased understanding and clarity.
- *Reserve judgment and have a tolerance for ambiguity.* Learning from data requires a tolerance for uncertainty and a willingness to live in the dissonance long enough to investigate and explore ideas until there is some clarity about what the data might mean.
- *Take a range of perspectives and systematically pose increasingly focused questions.* Data almost never provide answers. Instead, using data usually leads to more and more focused investigation and to better questions.

Data Literacy

There is probably nothing in education that garners more public attention than data about schools. However, interpretation and application of data by educators, and by the public, are often woefully inadequate, and sometimes downright wrong. Unfortunately, data in education have been equated with scores on large-scale assessments. When the only data that enter the conversation come from a single (and limited) source, the conversations are also limited and superficial.

As Hess (2008) says, student achievement data only yield a "black box" (p. 14). They illustrate how students are faring but do not enable the organization to diagnose problems or manage improvement. The scope and quality of evidence must be much broader and intentionally focused on the issues at hand. If school leaders are going to be active in interpreting and using data of all kinds, as well as challenging and disputing interpretations or uses that they believe are contestable, they must become data literate.

Data-literate leaders are those who do the following:

- *Think about purpose(s).* No doctor would take a patient's temperature and use it to ascertain his or her cardiovascular fitness; neither would pilots be content with speed as the only data needed to plan transatlantic flights. All too often, educational decisions are made using no data or available data, rather than appropriate data. Data-literate leaders realize that they need different data for different purposes.
- *Recognize sound and unsound data.* Data are numbers or words or pictures that represent some underlying ideas. They are estimates, with some degree of uncertainty, not absolute measurements. One of the first challenges for anyone interpreting data is to ascertain the quality of the data that he or she intends to use. Bad data can contribute to bad decisions. For some leaders, the existence of flawed data is sufficient reason to ignore or mistrust data altogether. But to blame the data is unreasonable. When people use words to make false claims or offer unreasonable ideas, we don't blame the English language. Rather than trashing all statements with numbers in them, a more reasonable response is to learn enough about the statistics to distinguish honest, useful conclusions from skullduggery or foolishness (Abelson, 1995).
- *Are knowledgeable about statistical and measurement concepts.* Data in education are generally measurements or records of something, often analyzed using statistics. But statistics strike fear into the hearts of many people. For the most part, educators have not seen statistics as a useful addition to their tool kit for decision making. Instead, statistics are either imbued with a magical quality of numerical "truth," or they are mistrusted as blatant attempts to distort or to manipulate an audience. Neither of these positions is defensible. Tests and statistical procedures have been developed to try to provide *estimates* of such invisible human qualities as achievement or creativity. Moreover, there are conventions and rules for the measurement of student achievement that are extremely important, especially when the results are being used to make significant decisions. If leaders are going to use data to enhance rather than distort educational decisions, they have a responsibility to understand the principles that underlie the statistics.

- *Recognize other kinds of data.* Although we often equate data with numbers, statistics are not the only kinds of data that leaders can use. Opinions, anecdotes, and observations are all acceptable as data. There are some criteria that need to be met, however, for something to qualify as data: It is not enough to troll about looking for perspectives that support an existing system of beliefs. Genuine inquiry requires that qualitative data also be collected in some systematic way and that they be organized and analyzed to allow various views to be expressed and incorporated into the interpretation.

- *Make interpretation paramount.* Data and statistics may provide the tools for measuring educational concepts, but the numbers are only as good as the thinking and interpretation that accompany them. Data do not provide right answers or quick fixes. Instead, they are necessary but not sufficient elements of the conversations that ensue. Data offer decision makers an opportunity to view a phenomenon through a number of different lenses, to put forward hypotheses, to challenge beliefs, and to pose more questions. Interpretation requires time, thoughtfulness, reservation of judgments, and open challenge of—as well as support for—ideas. Interpretation, then, is simply thinking—formulating possibilities, developing convincing arguments, locating logical flaws, and establishing a feasible and defensible notion of what the data represent.

- *Pay attention to reporting and to audiences.* Not only do data provide lenses for seeing more clearly, but leaders can also use data to explain and justify their decisions to those who care to know. Jaeger, Gorne, Johnson, Putnam, and Williamson (1993) found that reports prepared for parents about schools did not contain the information parents considered most important for them. They were also misinterpreted by 30 to 50 percent of the parents who received them. Attention to audience, presentation of data, interpretation, and key messages cannot be overlooked as essential elements in using data wisely.

Leaders have the challenge of convincing everyone who works in the school of the merits of using data for productive change and creating the conditions in which data can become an integral part of school decision making.

A Culture of Inquiry

Schools that are focused on professional learning, as a continuous and essential responsibility, have developed a culture of inquiry in which accountability is a process of using evidence to identify priorities for change, to evaluate the impact of decisions, to understand students' academic standing, to establish improvement plans, and to monitor and assure progress (Herman & Gribbons, 2001). This "internal accountability" is what drives professionals in routinely challenging existing beliefs and practices and in using data to make sense of their environment, as well as in thinking about their future. To accomplish such a dramatic shift in mind-set for an entire school, data must become a core part of school culture, even a topic of staff room conversation and classroom practice. Leaders have the challenge of convincing everyone who works in the school of the merits of using data for productive change and creating the conditions in which data can become an integral part of school decision making.

In order to create a culture of inquiry, leaders must do the following:

- *Involve others in interpreting and engaging with the data.* New insights don't happen by osmosis. They come from facing ideas that challenge familiar ways of viewing issues. They happen in the dissonance and in the construction of new and shared meaning. Leaders contribute to a culture of inquiry by providing opportunities for others to become inquiry-minded and data-literate. This means facilitating, sponsoring, mentoring, and convincing others to engage with and think about the data, even (and especially) when it is hard work.

  Fullan (1999) describes learning communities as places where "interaction inside and outside the organization converts tacit knowledge to explicit knowledge on an ongoing basis" (p. 16). All too often, however, "new insights fail to get put into practice because they conflict with deeply held internal images of how the world works" (Senge, 1990, p. 174). Data can offer a vehicle for investigating tacit knowledge as a means of refining and even transforming it as it is converted into explicit knowledge for use in making institutional decisions.

- *Stimulate an internal sense of urgency.* Data can be a powerful mechanism for refocusing the agenda or recasting the problem. No school is as good as it can be; there are always areas that deserve attention. Data become the window for identifying "what next" and instilling urgency as a way of unleashing the energy associated with embarking on a course of action that makes sense in fulfilling the moral purpose of schooling (Earl & Lee, 1998).

- *Make time.* Making sense of data and using them to come to a sense of collective meaning and commitment is not an overnight process; it doesn't happen in one fell swoop. Leaders and the people who work with them are going to need time, and lots of it—to think about the important issues, to decide what data are relevant and make sure they have them, to consider the data and try to make sense of them, to argue and challenge and reflect, to get more information, to argue and challenge and reflect again, to formulate and reformulate action plans, to prepare thoughtful and accessible ways to share their learning with the community, and to stand back to consolidate what they have learned. Fortunately, the time spent will be an investment in organizational learning and better decision making, but leaders have the task of managing this precious commodity to ensure that important things are done well.

- *Use "critical friends."* The idea of *critical friends* is a powerful one. Friends bring a high degree of positive regard, are forgiving, and are tolerant of failings. Critics, on the other hand, are often conditional, negative, and intolerant of failure. Critical friends offer both support and critique in an open, honest appraisal (MacBeath, 1998). As Costa and Kallick (1995) describe it, a critical friend is "a trusted person who asks provocative questions, provides data to be examined through another lens, and offers critique of a person's work, as a friend" (p. 154).

  External critical friends, with expertise in data collection, interpretation, and use, as well as sensitivity and the ability to listen and think on their feet, come without vested interests and can build trust and bring a dispassionate perspective. They can observe what may not be apparent to insiders, facilitate reflection on issues that arise, explain complex data in accessible ways, ask questions, probe for justification and evidence to support perceptions, and help reformulate interpretations. They are not afraid to challenge assumptions, beliefs, or simplistic interpretations in a nonjudgmental and helpful way. Critical friends are well placed to remind participants of what they have accomplished and to facilitate their movement toward the next goals.

OUR VISION OF THE FUTURE

In our vision of the future, data are the tools for thinking that educators use routinely, and collaborative inquiry is "a way of professional being." Educators who are inquirers will never announce that they "do" inquiry, thus separating the activity from their professional being. Rather, they might describe how they work—that is, the ways in which they inquire into their professional practice and the manner in which they are always striving to develop and expand their capacity to inquire. These educators, with their "inquiry habit of mind," locate and consider evidence to describe the current state of affairs, focus their thinking, stimulate their conversation, and challenge their ideas—always in the service of improved learning and success for students.

REFERENCES

Abelson, R. (1995). *Statistics as principled argument.* Hillsdale, NJ: Lawrence Erlbaum.

Barber, M. (2002, April 23). *From good to great: Large-scale reform in England.* Paper presented at Futures of Education Conference, Zurich, Switzerland.

Costa, A. L., & Kallick, B. (1995). Through the lens of a critical friend. In A. L. Costa & B. Kallick (Eds.), *Assessment in the learning organization: Shifting the paradigm* (pp. 153–156). Alexandria, VA: Association for Supervision and Curriculum Development.

Earl, L., & Katz, S. (2006). *Leading schools in a data-rich world: Harnessing data for school improvement.* Thousand Oaks, CA: Corwin.

Earl, L., & Katz, S. (2007). Leadership in networked learning communities: Defining the terrain. *School Leadership and Management, 27*(3), 239–258.

Earl, L., & Lee, L. (1998). *The evaluation of the Manitoba school improvement program.* Toronto, Ont., Canada: Walter and Duncan Gordon Foundation.

Elmore, R. F. (1996). Getting to scale with good educational practice. *Harvard Educational Review, 66*(1), 1–26.

Fullan, M. (1999). *Change forces: The sequel.* London: Falmer Press.

Fullan, M. (2006). *Turnaround leadership.* San Francisco: Jossey-Bass.

Gray, J., Hopkins, D., Reynolds, D., Wilcox, B., Farrell, S., & Jesson, D. (1999). *Improving schools: Performance and potential.* Buckingham, UK: Open University Press.

Hakkarainen, T., Palonen, T., Paavola, S., & Lehtinen, E. (2004). *Communities of networked expertise: Professional and educational perspectives.* Amsterdam: Elsevier.

Herman, J., & Gribbons, B. (2001). *Lessons learned in using data to support school inquiry and continuous improvement: Final report to the Stuart Foundation.* Los Angeles: University of California, Center for the Study of Evaluation.

Hess, F. (2008, December). The new stupid. *Educational Leadership, 66,* 12–17.

Jaeger, R., Gorne, B., Johnson, R., Putnam, S., & Williamson, G. (1993). *Designing and developing effective school report cards: A research synthesis.* Greensboro: University of North Carolina, Center for Educational Research and Evaluation.

James, M., & McCormick, R. (in press). Teachers learning to learn. *Teachers and Teacher Education.*

Leithwood, K., Louis, K., Anderson, S., & Wahlstrom, K. (2004). *How leadership influences student learning.* Chicago: American Educational Research Association.

Little, J. W. (2005). *Nodes and nets: Investigating resources for professional learning in schools and networks.* Paper prepared for the National College for School Leadership, Nottingham, UK.

MacBeath, J. (1998). "I didn't know he was ill": The role and value of the critical friend. In L. Stoll & K. Myers (Eds.), *No quick fixes: Perspectives on schools in difficulty* (p. 118). London: Falmer Press.

Nonaka, I., & Takeuchi, H. (1995). *The knowledge-creating company.* Oxford, UK: Oxford University Press.

Putnam, R. T., & Borko, H. (2002). What do new views of knowledge and thinking have to say about research on teacher learning? *Educational Researcher, 29*(1), 4–15.

Robinson, V. M. J. (2007). School leadership and student outcomes: Identifying what works and why (William Walker Oration). *Australian Council for Educational Leaders (ACEL) Monograph, 41.*

Senge, P. M. (1990). *The fifth discipline: The art and practice of the learning organization.* London: Century Business.

Stoll, L. (2004). *Networked learning communities as professional learning communities.* Paper commissioned by Aporia Consulting Ltd.

Stoll, L., & Earl, L. (2003). Making it last: Building capacity for sustainability. In B. Davies & J. West-Burnham (Eds.), *The handbook of educational leadership and management* (pp. 491–504). London: Pearson Education.

Stoll, L., & Fink, D. (1996). *Changing our schools: Linking school effectiveness and school improvement.* Buckingham, UK: Open University Press.

Stoll, L., Fink, D., & Earl, L. (2003). *It's about learning; and it's about time.* London: Falmer Press.

Supovitz, J. (2006). *The case for district-based reform: Leading, building, and sustaining school improvement.* Cambridge, MA: Harvard University Press.

Timperley, H., Wilson, A., Barrar, H., & Fung, I. (2008). *Teacher professional learning and development: Best evidence synthesis iteration (BES).* Wellington, New Zealand: Ministry of Education.

CHAPTER THREE

USING ASSESSMENT DATA TO LEAD TEACHING AND LEARNING

PETER W. HILL

This chapter addresses the future of assessment data in schools and the ways in which teachers, principals, and system leaders will use the data to transform teaching and learning. Right now, most schools are flooded with assessment data, but much of that data is of limited value in improving classroom instruction. (A useful discussion of the dilemma of "too much data but too little information for school leaders" appears in a series of articles in the December 2008/January 2009 edition of *Educational Leadership,* Vol. 66, No. 4, entitled "Data: Now What?")

Priority is attached to data that are used summatively to meet system- and school-level accountability requirements. Much less attention is paid to formative uses of data to improve teaching and learning, particularly at the school and classroom levels. Worse, summative assessment data are often promoted as having a formative value far beyond their actual utility.

The future lies in adopting a tri-level approach to data use that explicitly recognizes the different data needs of the system, school leaders, and classroom teachers, and places a much greater emphasis at all levels on formative uses of assessment data. This is a much-anticipated future, to be sure, but one that is only now beginning to coalesce into a viable modus operandi. The seeds of this future can be seen in current practice. Cutting-edge schools and school systems already have in place parts of the puzzle, though few, if any, have them all. However, a synthesis of existing and new "technologies" is emerging that promises to usher in an exciting era in the use of data in which classroom professional practice will become more sophisticated and able to support personalized learning.

The future lies in adopting a tri-level approach to data use that explicitly recognizes the different data needs of the system, school leaders, and classroom teachers, and places a much greater emphasis at all levels on formative uses of assessment data.

In outlining this synthesis, this chapter draws on a wide range of thought and practice, but especially on the author's own work with colleagues Michael Fullan and Carmel Crévola, as summarized in our book, *Breakthrough* (Fullan, Hill, & Crévola, 2006). In *Breakthrough,* we argue, among other things, that a necessary precondition to the creation of excellent schools is an alignment of purposes, processes, and incentives at different levels within the system. We were particularly concerned about securing this alignment among the school/community level, the district/regional level, and the state/federal level. When it comes to using assessment data to lead teaching and learning, it is imperative to go to the level where it matters most—namely, the classroom. And so, for the purposes of this brief account, I describe a tri-level approach in which the three levels are the system, the school, and the classroom. This is essentially the same approach adopted by Rick Stiggins and Dale Duke (2008), who have provided an excellent summary of the different kinds of decisions, audiences, and information needs at the institutional (system), organizational (school), and classroom levels.

The tri-level approach envisaged is represented in Figure 3.1 as a pyramid, with the school system located at the apex, but with more extensive data collection and use occurring at the school and classroom levels. Note that Figure 3.1 indicates a two-way (up and down) vertical flow of information among the three levels, as well as two-way flows horizontally within each level.

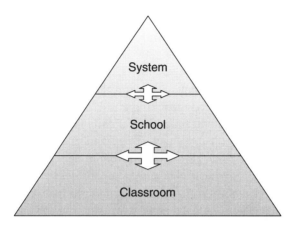

Figure 3.1   Tri-Level Representation of Data Use in School Education

At each of these levels, assessment data need to be used both summatively for accountability purposes and formatively for improving teaching and learning. The trick lies in getting the right balance at each level and ensuring the alignment of purposes and processes. Using assessment data *summatively* implies summarizing learning outcomes at the end of a defined period of time in the context of making a judgment about those outcomes. Using assessment data *formatively* implies monitoring progress at intermediate points in time for the purpose of generating feedback to inform midcourse adjustments. So let's now look at information requirements at all three levels, what the issues are, and the implications for leaders.

CLASSROOM-LEVEL DATA

The classroom is where instruction takes place and is the level at which the quality of educational schooling is determined. The classroom is also the level at which data can be most powerful in improving the quality of teaching and learning. In so many ways, these are self-evident truths, yet the reality is that for many years there has been little systematic attention to what actually goes on in the classroom. A transformation is underway, but it will take some time to materialize.

For too long, teachers have been left alone to pursue their craft behind closed doors, without any expectation that professional practice and the knowledge base of teachers were vitally important factors that needed to be constantly worked on in an open and collegial environment (see Burney, 2004). That situation is now changing rapidly, as schools are seeking to create professional learning teams in which teachers have opportunities to meet on a weekly or bi-weekly basis to focus on teaching and learning, and in which the deepening of professional practice is a daily occurrence as teachers work with a coach, observe each other, and give and receive feedback. At the same time, principals are being encouraged to reclaim the role of instructional leader and to regard quality of teaching as their main responsibility. These are overdue changes worthy of great celebration as the education profession as a whole experiences a sense of liberation and renewal.

Not coincidentally, these changes have come at a time when expectations of what teachers must deliver have never been greater. In the past, it was accepted that some students made good progress, the majority made satisfactory progress, and some made little or no progress at all. The Grade 8 teacher taught the Grade 8 curriculum, because after all these were Grade 8 students. For those students with little or no interest in academics, when they were through with school there were plenty of jobs that did not require high levels of education. The schools sieved out these students by the end of the compulsory period of schooling, and then settled down to focus on educating the more able.

But our world has changed. Low-skilled jobs have dwindled, and the Information Age and globalized economy have ushered in a world in which every person requires a high standard of education— not just to get and hold a job, but to participate meaningfully in the life of the community and to survive and flourish in a world of constant change.

The mission of schools has also changed dramatically, to one of educating *all* students to high standards and leaving *none* behind. This means that the teacher can no longer respond to a class of Grade 8 students as a homogeneous group to be taught in the same manner, but must instead treat them as a group of individuals in which the needs of *each* learner matter.

Personalizing learning is easy to say but hard to do, especially given the learning gap in today's typical classroom. By Grade 5, the gap between the top and bottom 10 percent of students of the same age is typically 5 years of schooling. By Grade 8, in an area such as mathematics, it may be as much as 8 years of schooling (National

Center for Education Statistics [NCES], 2007). So much for relying on the Grade 8 teacher knowing only the Grade 8 curriculum! *Every teacher needs to know what comes before and what follows.*

Personalizing learning is easy to say but hard to do, especially given the learning gap in today's typical classroom.

While content standards are appropriately age-specific, reflecting the maturity of the students and their age-related interests and experiences, performance standards can exist only as targets; we aim to assist as many students as possible to reach these targets, knowing that large gaps spanning several years of schooling may exist. The job of the teacher, always, is to establish each student's current location on the continuum of learning and to help students progress to a higher level as quickly as possible, but at a pace consistent with achieving mastery and deep learning. It is also the duty of the teacher (and of the school) to give extra time and support to those at risk of not achieving that level of proficiency necessary to cope with the requirements of the next level of schooling, in order to reduce achievement gaps.

This has been, I fear, a somewhat lengthy introduction to a discussion of classroom information requirements, issues, and implications. But it is critical. Only through the effective use of data can teachers hope to come anywhere close to being able to personalize the learning for each of their students. So, given the new mission of schools, what are the immediate information needs of the classroom teacher? They include the following:

1. A map of the objectives to be mastered for that part of the curriculum relevant to the students in the class (this will in all probability span several grades of schooling)

2. A profile indicating the location of each student for each objective on this curriculum map

3. A set of more detailed learning progressions or instructional pathways setting out the steps the typical learner will take in achieving mastery of each objective

The first of the above is typically available, though teachers have tended to restrict their attention to grade-specific objectives because the curriculum has been packaged content-wise rather than in terms of students' performance levels. The second information need, the student profile, must be obtained because it has not yet been incorporated into standard operating practice in most schools. This involves assessing students at the *beginning* of each school year to establish their starting points and to generate a profile of their strengths and weaknesses. Of course, if detailed records of students' attainment at the end of the preceding year are available, this assessment can be considerably simplified, but all too often such records are not available, and in any case are dated. Whether or not good records exist, schools need to establish data protocols that specify the kind of assessments that will be given at the beginning of the year, how the results will be used to generate student profiles, and how they will be used to create instructional groups within classrooms and to initiate instruction targeted at students' learning needs.

Next, in order to provide focused instruction, the classroom teacher needs to understand those more detailed steps taken by students in mastering a given objective. Cohen, Raudenbush, and Ball (2003) refer to them as "instructional sequences"; Popham (2008) refers to them as "learning progressions"; and in *Breakthrough* we refer to them as "instructional paths" (Fullan et al., 2006, pp. 54–55).

Let's consider an example. The performance standards for Grade 8 math might include being able to add, subtract, multiply, and divide rational numbers (including integers, fractions, and terminating decimals). But this subsumes a whole lot of content; for example, it includes being able to multiply two negative rational numbers. When I was in school, I was simply given the following rule: "When you multiply two negative numbers, the result is positive." Thus, $-2 \times -2 = 4$. I was not taught *why* the two negatives magically turned into a positive. These days, we expect students to understand why; as a result, there are steps we need to take that will enable the learner to understand the concept behind multiplying positive and negative numbers. Teachers need access to these steps; they should not be expected to reinvent them. Teachers should be free—indeed, encouraged—to devise alternative steps, of course, but not expected to function as though these were untrodden paths.

Armed with this kind of information, focused instruction can commence, assuming of course that teachers have adequate mastery of the instructional strategies appropriate for the different learning objectives they will pursue. Within the one class—and particularly in a mixed-ability language class—the teacher may need to organize three or four instructional groups needing different instructional foci. Now we come to the next set of information needs: The teacher needs to keep a record of each lesson.

In *Breakthrough* (Fullan et al., 2006), we illustrate how, in the context of early literacy, the necessary information can be collected through a one-page, all-purpose Focus Sheet, which the teacher can use to plan the lesson (both for the whole class and for specific small groups); specify instructional foci, resources, and instructional strategies; record the outcomes for those students the teacher has worked with and observed in individual or small-group settings; and record reflections on the effectiveness of the instruction provided. (An example is provided in Figure 3.2.) This Focus Sheet can readily be modified to suit older students and other subjects, such as middle school math. (Note that much of the information recorded by the teacher is qualitative. There is no need for scores or grades, only an indication of the extent to which the student has been able to demonstrate mastery of the content taught.) As well as being a planning tool, the Focus Sheet facilitates collection of all the information needed to track students' progress and to indicate where to take instruction in the next lesson. It also serves as a record of what was taught to each student, when it was taught, how many times, with what success, and over what period of time.

Along with analyses of student work, this is the information teachers need to manage the learning process, and to use formatively to adjust their instruction. Focus Sheets look quite different from the traditional teachers' grading or marking books, with their arrays of grades awarded to students for different pieces of work, and they are used quite differently. In addition to using them to track students and plan instruction, teachers bring their Focus Sheets to weekly or bi-weekly professional learning team meetings, along with examples of student work, where they share with their colleagues what has happened since the last meeting and problem solve together in areas where they are experiencing challenges. No more is the classroom (or, for that matter, meetings about administrative matters) a "black box": The focus remains relentlessly on a collegial approach to ongoing improvement of instruction, led by the data.

Probably midway through the year, and certainly at the end of the year, it will be necessary to summarize students' progress. We are now talking about using data summatively to report to parents, so school-level protocols are needed that specify what assessments will be given

Class: *1C*		Date: *9/28*

Whole Class

Title: Growing Mushrooms

Teaching Foci:

1. Formulate responses based on personal experiences.
2. Use picture clues to assist with unfamiliar words.
3. Produce phrased and fluent reading.

Small Group

Instructional Strategy: ○ Oral Language ○ Language Experience ○ Shared Reading ○ Guided Reading ○ Reciprocal Teaching	**Materials:** **Title:** Planting a Garden **Text Level:** E	Group 1	Tanya A.	David C.	Carlos E	Sam G.	Marcia H.	Chung K.
Instructional Foci	Formulate responses to author's message based on personal experiences, beliefs, and understandings of the world.		3	3	3	7	3	3
	Use a variety of strategies such as beginning, middle, and final letters, spelling patterns, word endings, etc. to problem solve on unfamiliar words.		7	7	3	3	3	7

Comments for Future Instruction: Tanya, David, and Chung all need more work in using a variety of strategies at the word level. Sara will benefit from staying in this group. Provide extra opportunities in learning centers to have these students work on vocabulary and word attack skills. Select another nonfiction text for a Read To in small-group session.

Whole Class

Share Focus: Articulate what you learned today that will help you as a reader.

Comments for Future Instruction: Need to make sure I allocate a share focus to students who are needing practice articulating their learning.

Figure 3.2 Example of a Focus Sheet for Reading K–3

and what information will be used for this purpose. Certainly the teacher's cumulative record of progress is part of that information, but there are likely to be other more formal assessment tasks, including tests, that the school will wish to administer—based on expectations for the relevant grade level, which the classroom teacher will be intimately involved in setting, administering, and marking—but this is really an issue for our next level of assessment data use: the school level.

In many school districts around the world, moderated school-based assessments are being used alongside test results to generate final assessments. This includes high-stakes examinations and assessments. It enables more authentic tasks to be used that can assess outcomes that are often difficult to assess through a paper-and-pencil test, such as the ability to research a topic and produce an extended piece of work. Linda Darling-Hammond and Laura McCloskey (2008) provide a useful summary of places where this is happening.

SCHOOL-LEVEL DATA

When it comes to teaching and learning, schools require assessment data to enable them to evaluate their performance as a school, to be accountable to parents for the progress of their students, and to manage teaching and learning within the school. Key questions to ask include the following:

When it comes to teaching and learning, schools require assessment data to enable them to evaluate their performance as a school, to be accountable to parents for the progress of their students, and to manage teaching and learning within the school.

1. What is the performance of the school, both relative to other schools and over time?

2. How are students performing?

3. What are students actually being taught, and with what success?

4. Which classrooms and which students need extra support?

The first of the above two questions involves making summative uses of assessment data, whereas the last two questions concern formative uses and cutting-edge practice.

For a school to evaluate its performance, the school system must provide timely, accurate, and balanced data on the performance of the school as measured by systemwide tests, relative to other schools and over time. It must also provide adequate tools and training to enable schools—especially the principal and senior staff—to interpret the data and communicate them in productive ways within the school community.

School systems in recent years have invested in the infrastructure needed to provide schools with detailed information on student performance on systemwide testing programs. Judicious use of these data can provide a picture of overall status and of progress over time, as well as an indication of strengths and weaknesses. The latter can be helpful and provide a focus for improvement efforts. Sadly, many schools have become convinced that if only they dig more deeply into the mass of data that is provided to them, they will discover many more nuggets of useful information to assist them in improving teaching and learning. Apart from the obvious problems arising from the fact that the data typically reach schools many months after the tests were administered and relate to a previous cohort of students (and indeed teachers), most accountability tests comprise relatively few questions and are thus able to provide little more than a general snapshot of students' strengths and weaknesses. Therefore, schools need to guard against over-interpreting or misreading the results from system-level testing programs. More will be said about these dangers when we look at system-level data.

The second of the above questions, "How are students performing?" needs to be addressed in the context of the school's need to account to parents. As just mentioned, at the end of the school year (and perhaps midway also), schools need to make a summative assessment of each student in a form they can communicate meaningfully to parents or guardians. This assessment usually takes the form of a set of grades (say, A through E), with one or more of the grades linked to systemwide performance standards and representing an absolute level of performance. But responsive schools typically provide additional information, such as the amount of progress students have made relative to their starting points at the beginning of the year (remembering that establishing starting points is a first priority in data collection in classrooms) and relative to other students within the school.

Any of these ways of referencing a student's performance involves a *summative* judgment about the point reached by the student at the *end* of the reporting period, and not at different points along the way. Schools thus need data protocols in place that set out the instruments, methods, and processes that will be used to generate these assessments. In many schools, particularly high schools, the default protocol has been for teachers to keep grading or marking books in which they have entered a grade for every assessment made of student performance; these grades are then averaged at the end of each reporting period.

This method of deriving a summative assessment conceals the end point actually reached by the student. It is generally a sure sign that no room has been left for formative assessment, or assessment designed to provide feedback to guide what Popham (2008) refers to as the "instructional adjustment" decisions of teachers and the "learning tactic adjustment" decisions of students (p. 11). It often indicates that assessment is being used as a means of accumulating a large body of evidence to justify the grade awarded, and perhaps also as an undeclared tool for controlling student behavior. It certainly indicates an overemphasis on summative assessment and a need for the school to institute protocols that strike a better balance.

Returning to our four questions, questions 3 and 4 are relevant to managing teaching and learning within the school. To answer them, and in order to drive improvement, good information is required. There needs to be ongoing monitoring by principals, teacher leaders, and teaching teams of what is being taught and learned and which classrooms require additional support. Stiggins and Duke (2008) suggest (and I agree) that this kind of information is required every few weeks, so the issue is, what does this information look like and how is it collected? Is it really feasible for the principal to be this well-informed without spending every minute in classrooms? The answer is, "Yes, quite simply." The solution lies in what we have already described: namely, teachers bringing to weekly or bi-weekly professional learning team meetings their Focus Sheets and their examples of student work for discussion. It then becomes the job of the coordinator of these meetings to summarize this information. What has this group of teachers been teaching? What issues have they encountered, and what actions have they planned? Which students are having problems with what, and in which classrooms is extra help needed? The coordinator needs to prepare a brief report that reflects the outcomes of these meetings and discuss the findings with the principal so that together they can take action.

This practice uses formative assessment data at the classroom level and filters it into key messages requiring school-level attention. It enables the principal to always have the big-picture view of teaching and learning in classrooms, to be responsive to emerging needs and problems, and to be focused when conducting regular classroom visits. It is not information that is used summatively to make judgments about teachers; instead, its purpose is always to enable necessary adjustments in the support made available to classrooms. And of course it is grounded in the belief that one cannot afford to wait until midway through the year, or until the end of the year, to find out that all is not well. One must constantly monitor students' learning and intervene as soon as one becomes aware of issues that could become problematic later on.

SYSTEM-LEVEL DATA

School systems need to account to the community at large for the performance of their students and schools, and to demonstrate the extent to which they are able to achieve both excellence and equity at a reasonable cost to the taxpayer. So educators need to use assessment data *summatively* as a means of evaluating how well their levels of performance compare with those of other systems, against standards and targets, and over time. However, they also need to use assessment data *formatively* to make adjustments to policies, initiatives, and resource allocations. Finally, they need to be actively involved in promoting assessment literacy and the effective use of assessment practices at the school and classroom levels.

In an increasingly globalized world, there are fewer compelling reasons why curricula, standards, and assessments should differ significantly from state to state within the same country, or even from nation to nation.

In the case of student learning, school systems typically obtain key assessment data through participation in national or international achievement surveys and by conducting their own system-level assessment programs. The technology for obtaining high-quality summative information on student learning is sophisticated, involving very special kinds of expertise in test construction, validation, sampling, scoring, and analysis, and generating issues and requiring decisions that are often obscure even to professional educators. For many school districts, the costs of obtaining and effectively managing the collection of such information can be burdensome, but they are also partly avoidable.

In an increasingly globalized world, there are fewer compelling reasons why curricula, standards, and assessments should differ significantly from state to state within the same country, or even from nation to nation. A better option can be cooperation and participation in national and international curriculum and assessment initiatives in which there can be a pooling of resources to obtain a higher-quality product. Large-scale, well-funded assessment programs will benefit from greater rigor in all phases of test construction, processing of results, and reporting of outcomes. In addition, the data are likely to have greater credibility and enable benchmarking against other systems.

This is the path currently being pursued in Australia, where after years of fitful attempts the states are finally working together with the federal government to pursue a national approach to curriculum and assessment. It is also the path being taken by a growing number of nations outside the Organisation for Economic Co-operation and Development (OECD) that have opted to participate in the Program for International Student Assessment (PISA; 67 countries are participating as of 2009). It is also a trend in the United States, where a number of initiatives promote collaboration among states, such as Achieve, an independent, bipartisan, nonprofit education reform organization that helps states raise academic standards and graduation requirements, improve assessments, and strengthen accountability.

Typically, school systems report outcomes of learning in terms of the percentages of students at or above a given level (e.g., "proficient" or "competent"), as represented by one or more cutoff scores on a test. This method of reporting results is commonly adopted because percentages are intuitive and readily understood in the community at large. But they are much more unstable and contain less information than, say, a mean score on a test. This is a serious issue in view of the high-stakes consequences of many testing programs. For many small schools, the degree of uncertainty or measurement error around the school's performance (typically expressed as the percentage of students meeting a given standard) turns out to be greater than the amount of change that the system has declared to be necessary in order to demonstrate adequate progress (typically expressed as a percentage improvement). As a consequence of the failure to understand confidence intervals, many schools erroneously conclude that they did very well one year but poorly the next, when in fact the differences were not statistically significant. In addition, some schools that put intensive effort into improving outcomes for those students expected to perform just below the cutoff score may succeed in increasing their "percent proficient" results but remain unaware that their mean scores are actually declining.

There are other undesirable effects of reporting results in terms of percentages of students meeting a given standard. Percentages can give a different picture of gaps and trends, depending on which part of the score distribution one examines (see Ho, 2008, for a lucid explanation of these problems). Assuming that performance has been measured on an equal-interval scale of ability (which it usually is), a small change in performance in the middle of the score distribution is likely to result in a substantial change in the percentage of students achieving the standard, whereas a large change in performance at either end of the score distribution is likely to be associated with only a small change in the percentage of students. Few educators appear to understand this important distinction, and the risks of poor decisions from not doing so are significant. The reports prepared by OECD on PISA results do not suffer from these problems, though they do report percentages at different levels, but not to measure trends or examine achievement gaps.

The most hazardous use of "percent proficient reporting" tends to occur in making judgements about the performance of schools and the progress of students. Schools can vary enormously in the composition of their student intakes; consequently, knowing the proportion of students at or above a given level is not enough to determine the performance of a school or the progress of students. Other data essential to take into account include the impact of student background characteristics and starting points.

Certainly district administrators need to know the absolute performance levels for the system as a whole, but at the school level it is also essential to know what value is being added over and above what students bring to school with them. Over the years, techniques for estimating, using, and reporting value-added indicators have been refined to the point where they should be adopted by all systems serious about evaluating the performance of their schools. Systems such as those in the state of Tennessee, the cities of Chicago and Dallas, and in England and Wales have been pioneers in the field (for further details, see Braun, 2006). The OECD (2008) report, *Measuring Improvements in Learning Outcomes: Best Practices to Assess the Value-Added of Schools,* is essential reading for those contemplating going down this path.

Obtaining information on the performance of schools raises the broader issue of the impact of school system accountability processes. Systems need to carefully balance pressure with support, creating incentives that maximize productive uses of data and minimizing and even eliminating unintended negative backwash effects. If the stakes are high, undesirable behaviors tend to follow, including excessive drilling of students on accountability tests and a host of other actions intended to "game the system." Those being held accountable may exploit all avenues to improve measured performance (Meyer, 1996). In so doing, they can subvert the outcomes that the accountability system was intended to promote, generate loss of confidence in the system, and diminish the validity and reliability of the assessments. On the other hand, accountability systems that manage to keep the focus on productive uses of information relevant to teaching and learning are likely to be successful in improving outcomes (see especially O'Day, 2002).

System leaders, therefore, need to think carefully about the incentives and disincentives that the system's assessment program will generate or has already created.

Openness, transparency, and frank discussion of the purposes of any accountability program are essential, so that both declared and perceived purposes can be aligned. There needs to be a climate of trust, rather than of misunderstanding and fear.

Openness, transparency, and frank discussion of the purposes of any accountability program are essential, so that both declared and perceived purposes can be aligned. There needs to be a climate of trust, rather than of misunderstanding and fear. Emphasis should be placed on persuasion regarding the moral purpose of the assessment program, an acceptance of personal accountability, and a focus on improving instruction.

An example of a high-performing system that has consciously sought to avoid excessive high-stakes accountability testing is that of Hong Kong, where there is annual testing of the basic competencies of all students in Grades 3, 6, and 9 in the Chinese language, the English language, and in mathematics (Hong Kong Examinations and Assessment Authority, 2008). Students are randomly assigned one of three or four versions of the test, each of which is equated so that all students receive an ability estimate on the same scale, and yet performance on a wide range of curricular objectives can be assessed. In addition, sample testing is conducted of students' oral language abilities in the two languages.

Results of individual students are not released, however, as this would make the testing very high-stakes, particularly given the intense concern Hong Kong parents typically display for their children's academic performance. In addition, schools receive their results only after signing a confidentiality agreement with the Education Bureau that neither party will release the results to a third party. What this means is that there is no publishing of "league tables" of school results in the local press. Each school receives detailed analyses of its students' performance via a secure Web site and is invited to send teachers to meetings to discuss student performance and strategies for addressing areas of weakness. In other words, considerable attention is paid to using the data formatively and designing the assessments so that there are sufficient data to pinpoint areas of strength and weakness.

School systems need to make formative use of assessment data and to promote them at the school and classroom levels. At the international level, PISA has provided compelling evidence regarding the effects of high student–teacher ratios, teacher salary levels, teacher quality, the impact of instructional leadership as exercised by principals, external standards-based assessment, and both student and school socioeconomic background on test scores (see Whelan, 2009, for a superb summary of factors revealed by PISA as influencing system performance). It has also challenged many beliefs regarding such practices as streaming and privatization of schools. School systems need to invest in careful analyses of their national and system-level data. This author was privileged to be a part of a national forum in Japan in June 2005 that took a long, hard, disarmingly open look at that country's performance on PISA; as a result of that meeting, senior decision makers arrived at profound conclusions regarding a new way forward.

The same applies at more local levels. Systems need to invest in collecting a range of supplementary data that might explain patterns of performance on systemwide tests and to invest time in analyzing and reflecting on the information such analyses can generate. For example, the York Region District School Board within the province of Ontario, Canada, is currently taking a hard look at its assessment data, including credit accumulation and graduation rates, and is planning to adopt a case management approach to assisting the relatively small proportion of students who are not successful on the Ontario Secondary School Literacy Test.

Finally, all school systems need to be actively involved in promoting assessment literacy and the effective use of assessment practices at the school and classroom levels. This includes making assessment tools available for use by classroom teachers and providing professional learning opportunities to school leaders and teachers on using ongoing formative assessment to provide instructional feedback to teachers and students. This is indeed the direction in which most U.S. systems are headed right now.

DATA FLOW AND ALIGNMENT

The power of assessment data in improving teaching and learning is never greater than when it flows both horizontally and vertically within a system in which there is alignment of policies and processes at all levels. This is what is intended by the horizontal and vertical arrows in Figure 3.1 on page 33. Let's consider what this means.

At the classroom level, it refers to the daily flow of information among teachers, students, and parents. It involves teachers giving constant formal and informal feedback to students on what they can do to adjust their learning. It also involves students reflecting on and sharing their responses to their learning within class—say, through the medium of a learning journal. To begin with, students may not have much to say; this changes rapidly, however, and students will astound teachers with their perceptiveness, their openness, and their capacity to give the teacher valuable insights that will assist him or her in fine-tuning instruction.

In many schools, teachers are exploring new ways of maintaining more ongoing contact with parents, particularly through the medium of email, but also by creating more informal opportunities to meet in the classroom after school. Such opportunities tap into the enormous potential for improved student motivation and support for learning through home–school partnerships.

At the school level, the expectation that a significant part of each weekly or bi-weekly professional learning team meeting will be devoted to the sharing of and reflection on assessment data generates insights, ownership, and personal accountability. This can be further enhanced when teams meet with colleagues from other schools in the context of an improvement initiative.

This is happening right now within eight district school boards in the Northern Ontario Education Leaders network. Teachers are constantly sharing and interacting with evidence of student performance and discussing it in both intimate and large forums. And they are all looking at the same data, so the conversations are more meaningful than if each school were collecting different data.

Another form of school-level sharing is the *data walls* that many elementary schools now maintain for use by faculty and educational leaders—summarizing the progress of each student, showing the relationships among different measures of attainment, and highlighting those students who need extra help. From Fresno, California, to Baltimore, Maryland, from the north of Canada to the Antipodes, schools are finding that keeping the data at the forefront of everyone's attention serves an important symbolic function in addition to its eminently practical importance.

For principals and school leaders, there is an ongoing need to promote the effective use of assessment data within the school. This may take time, as teachers move from a beginning stage of data use to the point at which they can be described as advanced users (see Figure 3.3).

At the system level, a big challenge right now is in promoting productive uses of assessment and related data. Most school systems have invested in the technology to collect and deliver data to schools and have solved problems of data storage and integration through building "data warehouses"—namely, large relational databases. Moving beyond mere bulk storage of masses of data to the generation of meaningful information is the next step; otherwise, the data stay in the warehouse, or somewhere inside the computer on the principal's desk. The toughest connection to make is the one between assessment data and instruction, which needs to be made explicit.

Stage	Characteristics
Beginning	Acquiring familiarity with assessment data and becoming data literate
Developing	Able to critically interpret available assessment data
Proficient	Collecting and using assessment data in a focused way to address pressing questions concerning teaching and learning
Advanced	Using data protocols to collect, analyze, and use assessment data to monitor and manage instruction and learning within the school

Figure 3.3   Stages of Development in Data Use

This calls for support staff and advisors who can help staff members at all levels make that connection, and act as data coaches to schools.

The other big challenge is to create alignment and balance at all levels within the system in assessment policies and practices. This requires systems to be more engaged in what happens in each classroom and in providing greater support to classroom teachers and schools in the daily work of assessing students. At the end of the day, it is the quality of the feedback that the teacher provides to her students, and the extent to which she can gain information that shapes how and what she will teach each student in the class tomorrow, that will determine how the system performs.

As ever, much remains to be done, but we must not underestimate how far we have come in a relatively short time.

As ever, much remains to be done, but we must not underestimate how far we have come in a relatively short time. There is widespread acceptance that sound assessment data is the key to generating vital information that can improve teaching and learning, and a growing appreciation of how this can be done in the context of personalizing education and ensuring high standards for all. Despite the challenges, there has probably never been a time when educators have had reason for greater optimism regarding the transformation of classroom instruction required to make this a reality.

REFERENCES

Braun, H. I. (2006). *Background paper: The use of value-added models for school improvement.* Paris: Organisation for Economic Co-operation and Development.

Burney, D. (2004). Craft knowledge: The road to transforming schools. *Phi Delta Kappan, 85*(7), 526–532.

Cohen, D. K., Raudenbush, S. W., & Ball, D. L. (2003). Resources, instruction, and research. *Educational Evaluation and Policy Analysis, 25*(2), 119–142.

Darling-Hammond, L., & McCloskey, L. (2008). Assessment for learning around the world: What would it mean to be internationally competitive? *Phi Delta Kappan, 90*(4), 263–272.

Fullan, M., Hill, P., & Crévola, C. (2006). *Breakthrough.* Thousand Oaks, CA: Corwin.

Ho, A. D. (2008). The problem with "proficiency": Limitations of statistics and policy under No Child Left Behind. *Educational Researcher, 37*(6), 351–360.

Hong Kong Examinations and Assessment Authority. (2008). *Territory-wide system assessment, 2008: Report on the basic competencies of students in Chinese language, English language and mathematics, key stages 1–3.* Hong Kong, China: Author. Retrieved August 19, 2009, from http://www.hkeaa.edu.hk/en/bca_tsa.

Meyer, R. H. (1996). Comments on chapters two, three, and four. In H. F. Ladd (Ed.), *Holding schools accountable: Performance-based reform in education* (pp. 137–145). Washington, DC: Brookings Institution.

National Center for Education Statistics. (2007, June). *Mapping 2005 state proficiency standards onto the NAEP scales* (NCES 2007–482). Washington, DC: U.S. Government Printing Office.

O'Day, J. (2002). Complexity, accountability, and school improvement. *Harvard Educational Review, 72*(3), 293–329.

Organisation for Economic Co-operation and Development. (2008). *Measuring improvements in learning outcomes: Best practices to assess the value-added of schools.* Paris: Author.

Popham, W. J. (2008). *Transformative assessment.* Alexandria, VA: Association for Supervision and Curriculum Development.

Stiggins, R., & Duke, D. (2008). Effective instructional leadership requires assessment leadership. *Phi Delta Kappan, 90*(4), 285–291.

Whelan, F. (2009). *Lessons learned: How good policies produce better schools.* London: Fenton Whelan.

CHAPTER FOUR

DATA

Institutionalizing the Use of a Four-Letter Word

EILEEN DEPKA

T he use of data by school systems is on the rise. Data related to state test results are increasingly available. The implementation of a variety of assessment tools is becoming more frequent. Embedding the use of data throughout district operations is often the goal, yet involving teachers in the constant and consistent use of data takes a concerted effort.

Although the pressure of federal accountability was the likely catalyst for increased scrutiny of data in school districts, that alone will not result in a sustained and effective use of data. It is clear that simply reviewing data will not have sufficient power to affect results. Something must be done as a result of the data. A systemwide focus on continuous improvement, with data as its foundation, is the key. Institutionalizing a system that requires data-based decision making will guide districts to increased success.

[D]ata are a means to an end. That end is increased student achievement. The method I suggest . . . is a targeted focus on continuous improvement.

This chapter will highlight key practices in creating a system that gives a purpose to data. The suggested steps can result in increased involvement of district staff, an advanced need for a variety of data, and the realization that data are a means to an end. That end is increased student achievement. The method I suggest herein is a targeted focus on continuous improvement.

The following steps create a path to follow when working to embed the use of data in the organization.

1. Set the Stage

2. Connect Data to a Purpose

3. Provide a Structure

4. Blame Not; Fear Not

5. Avoid Hasty Conclusions

6. Provide a Variety of Data

7. Level the Goals; Layer the Data

8. Make the Data Clear

9. Encourage Curiosity

10. Provide Collaboration Time

1. SET THE STAGE

The school or district leader must set the example for others to follow. Leaders can inspire others by their practices. Dependency on data can be the example and the expectation set. Setting the stage includes promoting the regular and systematic use of available data for all school or district processes. This would include professional development, purchases, practices, adoptions, and events.

Establishing a purpose for the use of data is vitally important. The need is typically recognized, but the practice of actually using data is often sporadic. The use of data needs to be a forethought—part of a plan.

Creating an expectation for the use of data does not require difficult practices. It requires the continuous use of two simple questions: (1) What do the data tell us? And (2) how will we know if we are successful? These two questions can begin to guide practices that include the use of data to make initial and continued decisions and to evaluate the effectiveness of purchases, practices, and programs.

Requests for purchases can be a good place to start. A building principal, for instance, should expect appropriate data to support the purchase of a new software program, and be able to include the data with a request for purchase. What data support the need? What data support a particular program instead of a competitor's program? Initiatives have the best chance of being effective when they are supported by a data-based need. Although intuition can be effective, data will result in an increased chance of success.

Setting the stage is a great start. But that alone will not reach the desired end.

2. CONNECT DATA TO A PURPOSE

Although it may seem obvious, data should promote action. Next steps should be a given, an expectation. Although viewing data is a noble exercise, if no action follows the event, then nothing was gained by the analysis.

Next steps are a natural part of data analysis. When data are reviewed, questions will be raised, conclusions will be drawn, and hypotheses will be formulated. But that is only the beginning. What will be done with what was learned? How will the system respond to the data? A conscious decision needs to be made to act on the findings. If the data call for action, yet inaction is the response, it should be recognized that inaction is also a conscious decision.

3. PROVIDE A STRUCTURE

A cycle of continuous improvement is beneficial when attempting to embed the use of data into district practices. It provides a structure within which a systematic process can be implemented. Each step of the process indicates tasks that need to be accomplished. The cycle creates a need for data, and a structure for expected next steps.

Such a cycle can be seen in Figure 4.1. In this cycle, there are four steps: analyze, plan, implement, evaluate.

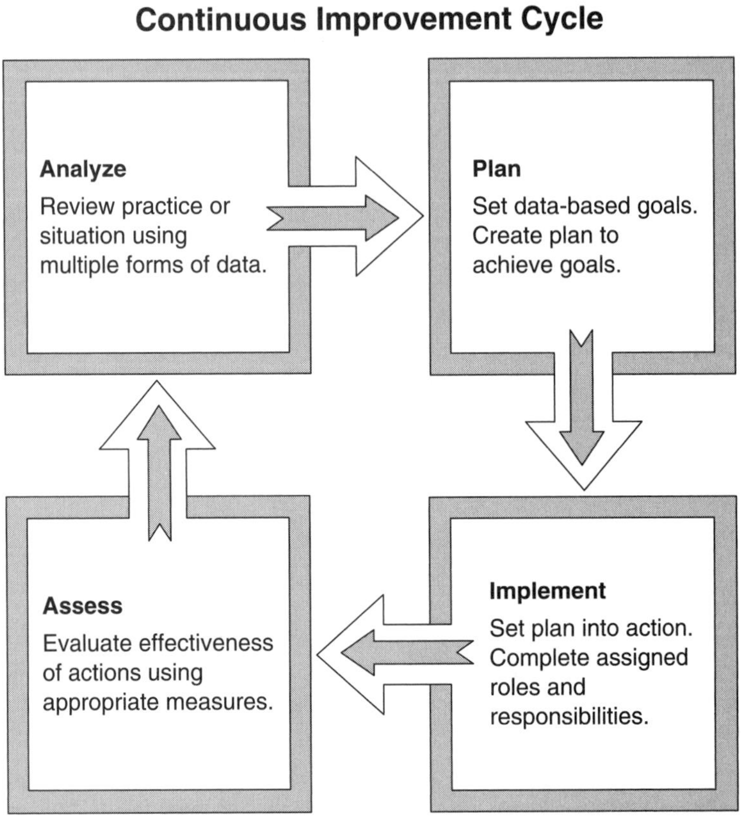

Continuous Improvement Cycle

Analyze
Review practice or situation using multiple forms of data.

Plan
Set data-based goals. Create plan to achieve goals.

Assess
Evaluate effectiveness of actions using appropriate measures.

Implement
Set plan into action. Complete assigned roles and responsibilities.

Figure 4.1   Continuous Improvement Cycle

During the *analysis* portion of the plan, data are reviewed. Student achievement data are most often the focus. During this phase of the cycle, it is important to view a variety of data. A well-rounded picture of achievement will provide the best chance for a valuable analysis. Data may include, but not be limited to, such national assessment results as AP, SAT, or ACT data; state testing data; and local common assessment data. The data should include disaggregations and a variety of levels of data depending on the purpose of the event. More information will follow in step 6.

The *planning* phase would typically begin with one to three goals based on the data analysis. The purpose of the planning phase is to create next steps supported by data to improve or enhance the current situation and achieve the goal(s). The plan would include a description of what will be done, by whom, and in what time frame to accomplish the anticipated results. Also needed are methods to assess the results and measure the effectiveness of the plan. Periodic data reviews will help measure progress toward the goals. Data analysis does not demand new goals, but may help to adjust the direction of current goals or action plans that were based on previously analyzed data.

All people within the organization should have ties to the goals and action steps. The focus should be broad enough so that all can take ownership of the goal, and all should feel that they can contribute to the successful completion of the plan. Although the goal needs to be focused so that it can be measured, the goal should be broad enough so that input, support, and action from all grade levels or departments are possible. What can art, music, and physical education teachers do to help support the goal? Can non-teaching staff have a role as well?

Losing sight of the plan can result in failure to achieve the goal. Losing sight of the goal can make the plan pointless. The plan should drive the organization.

The *implementation* phase is crucial to the effectiveness of the plan. Those responsible for various aspects of the plan have the responsibility to keep the goal at the forefront. Losing sight of the plan can result in failure to achieve the goal. Losing sight of the goal can make the plan pointless. *The plan should drive the organization.* Resources may need to be devoted to the plan. Professional development will be based on the goals and be part of the plan. New initiatives are put on hold and professional development is delayed, unless it is tied to achieving the plan. This type of focus will assist in balancing the workload and prevent teacher overload. As new tasks are recommended, this question needs to be asked of each: How does it fit into the existing plan, and in what time frame may it become part of the plan? If the fit does not exist, then the task is either eliminated or, if truly necessary, it is scheduled to take place at a suitable time. The plan takes precedence.

Assessment of a plan will likely take place at various times throughout implementation. With each assessment, the information should be cause for reflection and action. District common assessments, state assessments, survey data, and various other forms of information should be gathered and reviewed as available. The data also need to be reviewed collectively. One piece of data gives us a snapshot, but several pieces give us the album. Although each assessment will provide some information, multiple assessments will provide a more complete set of evidence from which the plan can be evaluated, conclusions can be drawn, and next steps can be formulated. Progress toward goals will also be measured through identified assessment results.

By definition, a continuous improvement cycle does not end. It is evaluated, reevaluated, perhaps tweaked, and the plan implemented again. Achievement of a goal may lead to higher goals, or the data may lead to the development of new goal areas. The expectation of the cycle remains, though. Data provide us with a direction; the plan creates the roadmap. The process is structured to analyze, plan, implement, assess, evaluate, and begin again.

A planning template is needed to document the plan. Complex, multiple-page plans may work for some. Simple, easy-to-follow templates have a greater chance at being living, breathing documents. *The magic is not in the document, but in the implementation of the action steps.* Figure 4.2 offers a suggestion for a template to be used during all phases of the continuous improvement cycle.

School:				Year(s):
Goal:				
Action Steps	**Person(s) Responsible**	**Important Dates**	**Cost of Action**	**Forms of Assessment**
Forms of Assessment Used to Measure Goal:				
Members of the Action Planning Team:				

Figure 4.2   Continuous Improvement Planning Template

With this example, each goal would require its own action-planning template. Actions listed would be tied to specific goals. The action steps are described clearly and concisely so that anyone who was not part of the plan's creation can understand it by reading it. The plan may span one year or several years.

Listing the person responsible is a key to the success of the plan. Who is ultimately responsible to ensure that an action is fully implemented? Completing the action may require the involvement of several individuals. The plan, however, need only list those with key responsibilities.

All dates important to the initiative should be included. When the plan is developed, it is understandable that dates may be tentative and certainly can be changed. Including the dates commits the team to action within a time frame and serves as a reminder that will help to ensure progress.

Although some actions may have no costs associated with them, others will require funding. Identifying and listing costs is important. If the cost is such that the action is not feasible, another action should be chosen. The plan should be written so that costs will not hinder its success. When action steps are necessary to reach the identified goal, yet include costly items, funding sources should be sought. Seeking funding should also be an action step included within the plan.

Methods of assessment should be identified as the plan is developed. Consider the success of each action step. What evidence will show that the step has been completed successfully? Evidence may consist of a document, a purchase, a professional development experience, a student assessment, or a variety of other possibilities. Other assessments used to measure progress toward the goal, but not necessarily associated with a particular action step, can be listed in the space labeled "Forms of Assessment Used to Measure Goal." This section of the template will be useful when preparing to analyze new data as they arrive.

Members of the action-planning team are listed on the plan. The efforts of this group have helped to move the organization forward, and the plan should recognize their participation. The names are also helpful when questions arise. Thought should be given to the makeup of the planning team in advance of their formation. When viewing the names on the action template, it should be obvious that a balance of individuals took part in plan development. An elementary school planning team, for example, would likely include teachers from a variety of grade levels, representatives who are content specialists, and an administrator. If a guidance counselor, social worker, or psychologist is part of the staff, this individual might join the team as well. Teaching assistants, parent representatives, and students are sometimes included on the team, depending on the school situation.

Providing a process and structure will promote data's consistent use. The use of data is a requirement of the process. Rather than a single event, data analysis will be an integral part of the continuous improvement planning process. The purpose of data use becomes increasingly clear and is embedded into a valuable system.

4. BLAME NOT; FEAR NOT

The intention of data analysis is to inform next steps. Open and honest evaluation requires a safe environment. Establishing an atmosphere of mutual respect and freedom from judgment is essential if data are to be analyzed effectively by the organization. Creating such an atmosphere takes a conscious effort and an unwavering example. An inherent fear that data will be used to reprimand or punish may exist in the organization, even if no specific instances have given rise to this fear. An increased use of data can cause such apprehensions to surface. Recognize the potential for fear and address the situation. Let educators know that data are needed to identify organizational strengths and challenges. Whatever is uncovered just *is*. What is *done* about the challenges should be the focus. Certainly causes should be identified, but causes are about practices, not about people.

Developing trust involves an attitude toward data that includes a philosophy that data simply *are*. Whatever is found is acknowledged.

The importance of the analysis is not in laying blame, but in finding a cure. If data analysis involves finger-pointing, or even the fear that it could take place, conversations and sharing are likely to end.

The importance of the analysis is not in laying blame, but in finding a cure. If data analysis involves finger-pointing, or even the fear that it could take place, conversations and sharing are likely to end.

Teachers need to be assured that the purpose of data analysis within the organization is to promote strengths and identify challenges in an attempt to incorporate both into processes of continuous improvement. If teachers are to work with the continuous improve-ment model, they need to feel that retaliation is not a goal. If poor practices are identified as a potential reason for questionable results, the practice, not the person, is the problem. Professional develop-ment may be part of the continuous improvement planning process.

Conversations are likely to be open and honest if the proper groundwork has been laid, and communication tied to data will increase. Action plans are more likely to be successful if discussions include difficult topics associated with challenging results.

5. Avoid Hasty Conclusions

The funny thing about data is that they often create more questions than answers. Additional data need to be sought in order to arrive at potential conclusions. A quick conclusion can be counterproductive and costly. A conclusion based on limited evidence may lead to an action plan that will have no impact on the results.

Encourage teams to view multiple sources of data before draw-ing conclusions. When data point in the same direction, there is a better chance that a successful action plan will be developed. After confirming that data support a course of action, the root cause of the data can be discussed and possible responses to the result can be brainstormed.

6. Provide a Variety of Data

Most districts have a wide variety of available data. It is helpful to create a data source designed to identify all assessment and survey tools used within the district. Figure 4.3 illustrates a template that can be used for that purpose. This simple list assists in identifying all major data sources, the grade levels and subjects affiliated with the data, the dates and times when assessments are administered, where the data are housed, and for what layers in the organization the data are available.

The time commitment for creation of a data source list is mini-mal. The tool will be beneficial any time new initiatives are imple-mented. When developing action plans, the source list helps identify tools already available that can measure the success of the plan or steps within the plan.

Type or Name of Source	Grade Level(s)	Subject or Survey Area	Months/ Years of Administration	Location of Data	Levels of Data Available		
					District	School	Class-room

Figure 4.3   District/School Data Source List

7. LEVEL THE GOALS; LAYER THE DATA

Effective data-based goals are developed at all levels of the organization. Goal development at the district level is based on broad district assessment results. In the schools, local data are viewed and may be compared to other schools within the district. At the classroom level, grade-level and subject-area results are processed. Individual student results are also analyzed. All levels of data can certainly be viewed by all levels of the organization. Goals are best developed using data that are closest to the specific layer of the organization. Figure 4.4 offers an illustration of the common levels of goals.

Goals developed at the district level are founded on broad-based data that include all students within the district. Data are analyzed, challenges are recognized, and goals are formulated. For example, if math scores are recognized as an area identified for improvement, a goal is formulated based on the desired results (perhaps a percentile) and the time frame (year) in which the results will be achieved.

School goals will support district goals because they are based on the data included in the districtwide database. The school needs to have freedom to create goals based on its specific needs; therefore, the wording of the goal may be different and may concentrate on a specific aspect. For example, the school may find that though there is room for improvement in its math results, the specific area of challenge seems to be that of problem solving. A goal dealing

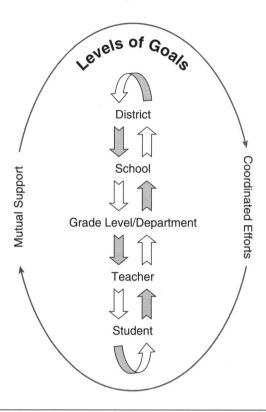

Figure 4.4   Levels of Goals

with improvement in that specific area will support the district goal, yet be designed to meet the needs of the school.

Grade-level and department goals are created to support school goals and to meet the needs of students within individual classrooms. Available data are used as a basis for goal creation. Data may not be available for all departments. Discussions are necessary to determine ways in which each grade level or department can support the school goals while meeting students' needs. The physical education department, for example, doesn't need a math goal to promote problem solving. The department would determine ways in which problem solving is needed within the physical education classroom and promote activities in which students will engage in problem solving related to physical education. Putting these plans in writing helps to create a higher level of commitment and organization to the building's planning process.

Teacher-level goals answer the question, "What will I do in my classroom to support and achieve the school goals?" That question is posed to every teacher in the school. The schoolwide action-planning template will also provide a format for classroom goals. Action steps are likely to be limited and could include just a few steps that are incorporated into activities throughout the school year.

Creating a student awareness of school and classroom goals is essential if students are to make a conscious effort to assist in goal achievement. A regular process of reflection can be used with students during which they analyze their current performance and determine the next steps needed in an effort to improve. Each teacher's action plan would include a commitment to providing time for this process.

The arrows in Figure 4.4 indicate that all plans are mutually supportive. All plans are based on the same data. Administrators would benefit from evaluating the connectedness of the plans and ensuring that district plans support actions being taken at other levels within the organization.

Although some data are needed at all levels within a district, all data are not needed at all levels. Choosing the appropriate data assists in making data analysis valuable, yet manageable.

Data required within the organization are directly tied to the levels of goals mentioned previously. Although some data are needed at all levels within a district, *all* data are not needed at all levels. Choosing the appropriate data assists in making data analysis valuable, yet manageable.

The layers within the organization pictured in Figure 4.4 are connected to the district, yet all require different data. In order to make an efficient and effective use of time and talent, decide the layers of data needed by various levels within the organization. Define the purpose of each data-analysis session. Provide data that are directly related to the specific layer of the organization, and include information that will guide action planning. Have additional data available in case they are needed.

When data are reviewed for district purposes, the analysis needs to include broad, district-level information. The analysis needs to give a complete picture of district performance. This process would likely include the performance of each school, but detailed student information would not be needed for this evaluation.

Schools need to have a good understanding of how they compare to other schools in the district and how their performance affects that of the

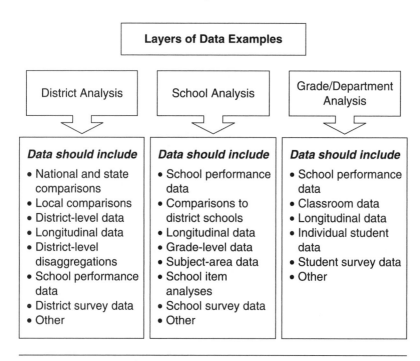

Figure 4.5   Layers of Data Examples

district as a whole. More important, schools need to have a complete compilation of their own specific information, including grade-level and subject-area results. Grade-level and department data will be more specific to the classroom and need to include detailed student information.

Figure 4.5 provides an example of how data can be layered to meet the needs of a specific group. Data should be chosen prior to completing an analysis session. Previously developed action plans will help guide participants toward the data that will be most effective for their purposes. The group analyzing data should also have input into what will be available during any data-mining session.

8. MAKE THE DATA CLEAR

School systems hire knowledgeable and effective educators who are experts in their field. Dedicated teachers and administrators alike work relentlessly to meet the needs of their students. When it comes to data analysis, however, *it is important to know the group*. In order to embed the use of data at all levels of the organization, data need to be provided in a format appropriate to the users. The majority of those who need and want to use data in a district are practitioners, not statisticians. Presentations of data require a style that is meaningful and easily understood. That is not to say that individuals cannot grow in their skills of data analysis. Identify an appropriate comfort level, supply the data, and routinely check for understanding. During a group analysis, each group leader should take the time to clarify the data and guarantee a level of understanding.

Multiple representations of the same data can provide views to meet the needs of most within the organization. That doesn't mean that more complex analyses should be eliminated. Those within the district who find data intriguing or have the role of data analyst can provide information for others. The goal is to keep all practitioners interested in data analysis by presenting complete, well-rounded data in a user-friendly format. Although it takes time to report data in a format in which it may not have originally been supplied, it is time well spent if the data can be reported clearly and concisely.

In order to make disaggregated comparisons easier to analyze, consider placing them on a single page. This does not need to be done prior to an analysis session but can take place during the analysis. Often disaggregations need to be viewed by comparing information on multiple pieces of paper. Figure 4.6 provides an example of a way in which the data can be reported on a single page. This template will allow comparisons between subgroups within and across years.

Different methods for reporting data can provide variations that assist in the interpretation. A chart can be used to record information. A graph of the same information can provide a different view. By using alternate views, data reviewers will recognize various formats that present specific information most effectively for their purposes.

For example, when completing an analysis of a district writing common assessment, several representations of data are required, depending on the level. The performance levels of each school are needed for analysis at the district level (and probably would be a welcome addition to a data review within individual schools as well). Figure 4.7 illustrates the results of a rubric-scored assessment. This presentation reflects the performance of each school on each trait of writing evaluated by the assessment—a level of detail that is useful at the district level for action planning. Each school will use the data

Assessment:

School:

Subject:

Year	All Students	Grade							Ethnicity					Lunch Status		Disability		Migrant Status		Gender	
		3	4	5	6	7	8	HS	API	A	B	H	W	Econ. Dis.	Not	Y	N	Y	N	M	F

Figure 4.6 Assessment Analysis Grid

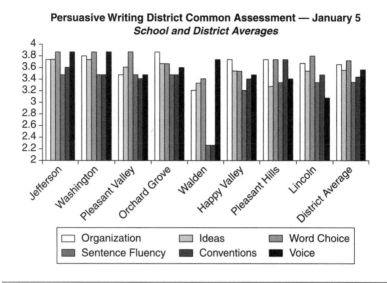

Figure 4.7   Persuasive Writing District Common Assessment: School and District Averages

to compare their results to those of other schools within the organization. Comparisons such as this can lead to discussions that concentrate on the sharing of best practices.

A graph such as Figure 4.7 can supply a great deal of information. The schools can be compared, using a single trait, by identifying the shade of the bar and looking across the graph at that particular trait. All traits within a school can be compared to identify strengths and challenges. Schools can then use the additional information to identify a school with strengths they lack. They can arrange to confer with that school to discuss practices that have led to positive results. Each school can also be compared to the district average. In addition, district strengths by trait can be identified.

Encouraging schools to look at districtwide results by school does assume that staff members are ready to collaborate. The results need to be looked at with the intention that future discussions will occur, including the sharing of best practices. (Note: Teachers will require more detailed information to make a difference within their classroom.)

If schools are not ready for that level of detail of districtwide information, at least the individual school results can be reported along with the district average. This will provide a measure of comparison necessary to add meaning to the data. Figure 4.8 is an example based on the same district-level writing assessment.

A chart is another method of reporting the same information found in Figure 4.8. Because there are several numbers within a chart, analysis can be confusing. Highlighting certain results can be used to create a meaningful picture. For example, all scores below the district average can be highlighted. Such emphasis makes it easier to see if specific students are having difficulty. One can also observe if the highlighting indicates difficulty with a particular writing trait.

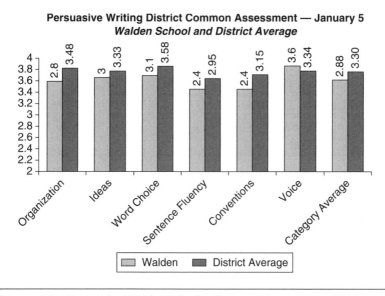

Figure 4.8   Persuasive Writing District Common Assessment: Walden School and District Average

Figure 4.9 provides a look at the same writing data. The lowest score for each student is highlighted. This can also shed light on strengths and challenges connected to specific writing traits. The chart shows that sentence fluency is an area in which student performance is low nearly districtwide. This would be a good topic of conversation when dealing with school and district improvement planning.

Teachers require data specific to their students if they are truly to see a need for data and grow accustomed to using them on a regular basis. Student data can be provided in formats similar to those in previous examples. Charted information would include student

	Organization	Ideas	Word Choice	Sentence Fluency	Conventions	Voice	Category Average
Jefferson	3.6	3.6	3.8	3.2	3.4	3.8	3.57
Washington	3.7	3.6	3.8	3.2	3.2	3.8	3.55
Pleasant Valley	3.2	3.4	3.8	3.2	3.1	3.2	3.32
Orchard Grove	3.8	3.5	3.5	3.2	3.2	3.4	3.43
Walden	2.8	3	3.1	2.4	2.4	3.6	2.88
Happy Valley	3.6	3.3	3.3	2.7	3.1	3.2	3.20
Pleasant Hills	3.6	2.9	3.6	2.8	3.6	3.1	3.27
Lincoln	3.5	3.3	3.7	2.9	3.2	2.6	3.20
District Average	*3.48*	*3.33*	*3.58*	*2.95*	*3.15*	*3.34*	*3.30*

Figure 4.9 Rubric Data Organized by School

names. The color-coding system can be used for data interpretation. Shading is used in Figure 4.10 to highlight all scores below the expected proficiency level of 3. The shading can help teachers easily identify students who are struggling. The shading also makes it easy to analyze specific traits.

	Organization	Ideas	Word Choice	Sentence Fluency	Conventions	Voice	*Student Average*
Martin	4	3	4	3	3	3	*3.3*
Jordan	4	3	3	3	3	3	*3.2*
Marie	4	3	4	3	2	3	*3.2*
Rosalita	4	3	4	3	2	4	*3.3*
Miguel	4	4	4	3	3	4	*3.7*
Jeremiah	3	4	2	2	1	4	*2.7*
Mia	3	3	3	3	3	3	*3.0*
Tyrone	4	3	4	3	3	3	*3.3*
Reggie	3	3	4	3	2	3	*3.0*
Mary	4	3	3	2	2	4	*3.0*
Category Average	*3.7*	*3.2*	*3.5*	*2.8*	*2.4*	*3.4*	*3.2*

Figure 4.10   Rubric Data Organized by Student

A graph of trait averages can provide a useful tool for quickly comparing classroom performance on each trait. Figure 4.11 creates such a picture. The information can be used by Mrs. Jendusa to plan lessons to assist in increasing student performance. Sentence fluency and conventions will likely require additional class time and opportunities for students to apply their skills.

Comparative information is also helpful when interpreting classroom data. Students can be compared to a class average as illustrated in Figure 4.12.

Specific student information can be viewed effectively in a bar chart, which allows areas of student strength (and areas in which students are having difficulty) to be pinpointed. Figure 4.13 can be used to visualize the data and use it to adjust future lessons. Much

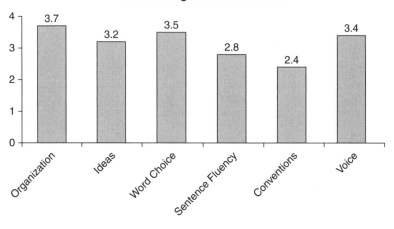

Figure 4.11   Persuasive Writing District Common Assessment: Class Averages for Mrs. Jendusa

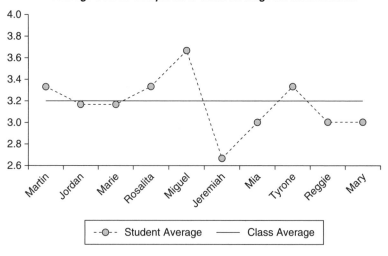

Figure 4.12   Persuasive Writing District Common Assessment: Average Scores Compared to Class Average for Mrs. Jendusa

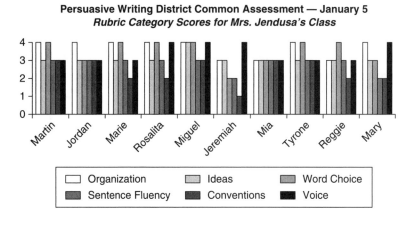

Figure 4.13 Persuasive Writing District Common Assessment: Rubric Category Scores for Mrs. Jendusa's Class

can also be learned about individual students. Jeremiah, for example, shows some real strengths. He scored the highest rubric value when evaluated for ideas and voice. He struggles, though, in word choice, sentence fluency, and conventions.

Results pictured on the graph can also be useful when creating flexible groups of students. Data show that conventions are an area of struggle for Marie, Rosalita, Jeremiah, Reggie, and Mary. Teachers can respond to the need, perhaps through specific instruction or differentiated lessons. Students should be privy to the information in Figure 4.13; it is essential that students be able to identify their areas of strength and to set goals to grow in areas of challenge.

Varied representations of data increase the likelihood that interpretations will be successful. When data are understood and used effectively, the demand for data will increase. Teachers and administrators will internalize the need for data. Based on the examples provided above, staff members will create their own representations of data, and the use of data will be expanded.

When data are understood and used effectively, the demand for data will increase. Teachers and administrators will internalize the need for data.

9. Encourage Curiosity

As stated previously, data often lead to more questions. Additional information may be needed to answer questions; typically, even more inquiries are likely to be identified. When questions are encouraged, data can be understood on a deeper level. Easily accessible data is an important part of this equation. Placing data at teachers' fingertips will increase their ability to analyze data and encourage them to delve well beyond surface-level data. A central data warehouse has the power to supply quantities of useful information and is a valuable tool worth considering. Queries can be created and information accumulated quickly and efficiently.

When data are made easily accessible, an "I Wonder" activity can be beneficial. "I Wonders" are questions generated when viewing data. The point is to continue to dig deeper into the data and find reasons for the results, as well as indications that point to effective actions.

Assume, for example, that the state reading results are shared and the data show that 35 percent of the students struggled with the test. An "I Wonder" session generates questions that aim to learn more about that 35 percent. Questions could include the following:

- Does the length of time students are in the district affect their performance on the test?
- Is the absentee rate higher for students who are not proficient on the test?
- What percent of students in each group previously received reading interventions?
- How does each subgroup perform when results are disaggregated?
- Did students from some schools do better than others?
- How does this performance compare with the same cohort group in other years?
- Did students who performed poorly on reading also struggle in math?
- What is the classroom performance in reading of those students below proficiency?

These questions and others can lead to an effective analysis of the original data and provide details useful in the creation of an improvement plan.

If data are available, no question should be discouraged. The answer may lead to steps that prove beneficial to students. Data need to be accessible to those asking the questions. Staff members need to be trained to compile data using various tools that house data sources. If that is not possible, data need to be made readily available by those with access to the necessary information.

10. Provide Collaboration Time

Data analysis and planning for continuous improvement take time. Certainly it is time well spent, given its potential impact on district and school performance. A commitment to providing time for collaboration has a direct link to increased use of data.

An expectation for increased usage of data will go only so far if time is not allotted regularly for that purpose. A yearly scheduled review of all district school data and improvement plans is a great start. Providing the opportunity for data review periodically throughout the year is also beneficial. The more data are viewed, the more likely they are to be used. The scheduling of purposeful data-based discussions supports a data-rich, data-dependent environment.

Productive collaborative time will result when an agenda is set and the purpose is clear. Group leaders need a clear picture of the intention and expected outcome of the collaborative experience.

Conclusion

Connecting the dots between data reviews and continuous improvement planning provides a clear guiding purpose for the consistent use of data. The need for data is recognized when it is an integral part of daily activities and when it is seen as clearly connected to school improvement. The realization that successful action plans are data-based and mutually supported assists in the continued use of high-quality evidence. Institutionalizing the use of data requires an expectation, a purpose, and a plan.

CHAPTER FIVE

USING DATA TO DRIVE INSTRUCTION AND ASSESSMENT IN THE STANDARDS-BASED CLASSROOM

KAY BURKE

THE POWER OF DATA

Today's educators are using data to drive instruction and improve student achievement. Almost all the processes in this age of accountability involve data because it requires self-analysis and supports the use of effective innovations and strategies. Schmoker (2001) says, "A rapidly growing number of schools have made a momentous discovery: When teachers regularly and collaboratively review assessment data for the purpose of improving practice to reach measurable achievement goals, something magical happens" (p. 1). These teams of teachers, however, will be more successful if they review data from common assessments they have created together and have used with their own students. When they meet to examine their students' work, they collect, analyze, and interpret the data and make decisions about how they plan to differentiate their instruction and reteach as needed to help all students succeed.

Even though the analysis of data is vitally important for making educational decisions, sometimes there is a difference between the data derived from formative classroom assessments collected by teachers and the data collected from the results of summative high-stakes standardized tests. One problem arises when teachers focus on the curriculum covered in their textbooks instead of on the concepts embedded in state standards. Educators post state standards in their classrooms, require students to identify the standards on which they are working, and provide both interim (benchmark) and final reports describing how students meet and exceed the standards. Sometimes, however, attention to the standards does not go much further than that. The posting of standards in a classroom does not necessarily mean that standards-based teaching and learning is occurring. Standards-based teaching occurs when teachers embed the *language of the standards* (LOTS), which includes the vocabulary words, people, events, and concepts from their state standards, into curriculum, instruction, and assessment; moreover, they must monitor students' progress in meeting and exceeding the standards through both formative and summative classroom assessments. If these valid standards-based assessments are used to provide teachers with data that redirect their instruction to help all students succeed, then data truly do drive both instruction and assessment.

The posting of standards in a classroom does not necessarily mean that standards-based teaching and learning is occurring.

FORMATIVE AND SUMMATIVE ASSESSMENTS

The data that teachers collect from formative classroom assessments and the data collected after students take summative high-stakes tests should be similar. If teachers have created lessons and assessments using the *language of the standards,* if they embedded the vocabulary words, people, events, concepts, and overarching (or enduring understandings) of the standards into their curriculum, instruction, and assessments, then the results of their classroom assessments should predict students' scores on standardized tests. The focus in many classrooms, however, is on teaching to the textbooks and the ancillary materials provided by publishing companies rather than to the state standards. Often the *language of the standards* from each state is not the same as the *language of the textbooks* published by textbook companies (which target adoptions in multiple states). When teachers base their instruction and their classroom assessments solely on the vocabulary words used in the textbooks, students may do well on their classroom assessments but score poorly on the state's high-stakes standardized tests that determine adequate yearly progress and promotion to the next grade.

The language used in all formative classroom assessments *should* be the language of the state standards. That same language should be used in all summative classroom assessments because the state tests are, or should be, correlated with the state standards—not the textbooks published by several companies and adopted by separate school districts throughout the state. Figure 5.1 shows the *balanced assessment model,* wherein the language of the standards is embedded in both formative and summative assessments so that classroom assessments become a more accurate predictor of student success, not only in individual classrooms but also on the high-stakes state tests.

When teachers embed the language of the state standards in all formative and summative assessments as well as in teacher-directed lectures, class discussion, group work, and individual work, students become familiar with the terminology and learn the related synonyms needed to improve their own vocabulary and their comprehension. They also are better prepared should they move to different states or countries where the educational standards may vary in terms of grade level, competencies, and language.

COMMUNITY OF LEARNERS

According to Little, Gearhart, Curry, and Kafka (2003), "organizations engaged in professional development and school reform have started bringing teachers together to do *collectively* what they generally do alone; that is, look at student work and think about

Formative Assessment	Summative Assessment
The Language of the Standards should be embedded in all	The Language of the Standards should be embedded in all
• Curriculum Units • Lesson Plans • Instructional Strategies • Formative Assessments • Common Assessments	• Scope and Sequence Plans • Benchmark Testing • State Standardized Tests • Summative Assessments • Common Assessments
Formative Assessments	Summative Assessments
• Informal Teacher Questioning • Conversations With Student • Informal Observations • Rough Drafts of Written Work • Learning Logs (in progress) • Reflective Journals (multiple drafts) • Mathematics Problem-Solving Steps • Practice Science Experiment • Rehearsals of Presentations • Working Portfolios • Practice Checklists for Do-Overs • Practice Rubrics • Homework, Quizzes • Benchmark/Interim Tests	• Formal Oral Interviews • Conference With Student • Formal Observations • Final Copies of Written Work • Final Learning Log Entries • Final Journal Entries • Mathematics Final Solution • Final Science Experiment • Final Presentations • Showcase Portfolios • Final Checklists • Final Rubrics • Teacher-Made Tests • High-Stakes Standardized Tests

Figure 5.1   The Balanced Assessment Model

SOURCE: Used with permission. From *Balanced Assessment: From Formative to Summative* (in print) by Kay Burke. Copyright 2010 by Solution Tree Press. All rights reserved.

students' performance in the classroom. . . . [T]he purpose of these collaborative efforts is to foster teacher learning" (p. 185, emphasis added), which in turn fosters student learning. A professional community provides a spirit of collaboration that encourages teachers to work with other teachers, special education teachers, support staff, curriculum specialists, and administrators to achieve a common goal.

DuFour (2004) describes a professional learning community as a systematic process in which teachers work together to analyze and improve their classroom practice. He believes that the professional learning community model focuses on the core mission of education: student learning. Instead of emphasizing what the teacher taught, the emphasis is instead on what the student learned. DuFour believes that every professional in the school building must engage colleagues in the ongoing exploration of three crucial questions that drive the work of those within a professional learning community: (1) What do we want each student to learn? (2) How will we know when each student has learned it? and (3) How will we respond when a student experiences difficulty in learning? (p. 8). When teachers collaborate to find out the answers to these three critical questions, they engage in rich conversations that guide both their instruction and their assessment.

New research is showing that strategic planning done by "planners" *before* the school year begins is not as effective as planning done by teaching practitioners *throughout* the school year. Schmoker (2004) believes most productive thinking is "continuous and simultaneous with action—that is, with teaching—as practitioners collaboratively implement, assess, and adjust instruction as it happens. The most productive combinations of thought and action occur in team-based, short-term experimental cycles" (p. 427). When teachers meet regularly to examine student work, analyze the data, and determine ways to differentiate their instruction so that all students can learn, they work as a team to meet the challenges of standards-based teaching and learning.

POWER STANDARDS

Reeves (2003) was one of the first educators to use the term "power standards" to describe important standards that teachers should select based on certain criteria. Reeves believes that the power standards should have *endurance* because they are skills that will last throughout students' academic careers and beyond. He believes in the principle of leverage because the standard is used in multiple courses and in multiple grades. Key standards such as informational reading and writing, mathematic relationships, scientific inquiry, oral communication, and thinking skills endure because they are threaded throughout the curriculum and grade levels. They represent critical skills that students will use throughout school, the workplace, and life.

Power standards cross into other curricular areas more often than regular standards. For example, students may learn *informational writing skills* in language arts class, but they use those research, writing process, and usage skills to prepare reports in social studies, science, art, music, and foreign language classes. In addition, teachers meet to decide which standards become "building blocks," or essential learnings for the next level or course. A mathematical understanding of *fractions* may be first taught in early elementary school, but it is revisited throughout math courses in middle school and high school. Therefore, an understanding of fractions is critical for helping students form a foundation of key mathematical concepts. Ainsworth and Viegut (2006) recommend that teams of teachers vertically align the power standards from one grade or course to the next to ensure that they represent a logical and comprehensive "flow" of instructional sequence from kindergarten through Grade 12. Schools or districts often develop curriculum maps to determine when all standards are to be taught and assessed during the school year. The data teams also analyze state tests to see which standards are emphasized most frequently. Analyzing the most important standards helps teachers focus on the big ideas and essential learnings, since it is almost impossible to cover *all* the standards and descriptors at each grade level, even superficially.

The teams then examine the *language* of their state standards. Teachers can no longer use only the terminology in their textbooks, workbooks, or assignments from Internet sources. The language in those resources may not correlate with the language used on high-stakes standardized tests that all students must take (and pass) in order to be promoted to the next grade or to graduate.

Vocabulary can be confusing, and students who must recognize the "base" word in their daily reading lessons may be confused when the state test requires them to identify the "root" word. Some students may be able to recognize that *base* and *root* are synonyms, but others may miss several questions. Here is another example: Students who draw "circle graphs" in math class may be able to understand that they are the same as "pie graphs" on the standardized tests, but they also could miss several test questions if they don't figure out that the two terms are essentially the same.

Many teachers display key vocabulary words on posters throughout their classrooms. They sometimes call these signs *word walls,* and their purpose is to help students review important concepts. These words, however, could be taken from the textbook and thus provide only *kid-friendly* definitions to help students remember the words and their definitions. Of course, it is important to provide students with developmentally appropriate definitions in the beginning of the year, but teachers need to eventually correlate the words and the definitions with the language in their state standards before students take the state tests. For example, the textbook may use the term *greeting* when referring to the beginning of a friendly letter. The teacher may put the word *Dear* in parentheses under the word *greeting* to help students understand the meaning. The teacher should also put the word *salutation* on that same sheet, however, because that is the word used in the state standard and will be the word used on the state test.

Vocabulary is critical for student understanding. When teachers use the words of the standards, they not only expand their students' vocabulary but also prepare them to take state standardized tests.

Vocabulary is critical for student understanding. When teachers use the words of the standards, they not only expand their students' vocabulary but also prepare them to take state standardized tests. Effective teachers use multiple synonyms in their classroom discussions and their formative classroom assessments so that students will be able to recognize the concept, regardless of their textbook, teacher talk, or the standardized test. Figure 5.2 shows how the vocabulary words used by teachers and textbooks in the classroom could be different from the words used on state tests.

Teacher/Textbook	State Test
Types of Literature	Genre
Circle Graph	Pie Graph
Thesis Statement	Focus Statement
Main Character	Protagonist
Base Word	Root Word
Rename	Regroup
Verb	Predicate
Compare/Contrast	Similarities/Differences
Closure	Clincher
Noun	Naming Parts
Time-Order Words	Transitions

Figure 5.2   Vocabulary Words

DIFFERENT STATES, DIFFERENT STANDARDS

Teachers must pay close attention to the *language of the standards* because the language can differ from state to state. Numerous Internet sites provide checklists and rubrics for assignments in all subject areas and grade levels. Many teachers are thrilled to find sites that showcase "rubrics from around the world," and they download and print them to use with their students. Often these checklists and rubrics are quite good, but they need to be "tweaked" to substitute the language of one state's standards with the language of the state in which the teacher works. Until the United States adopts national standards, each state is developing and testing its own standards. Teams of teachers in a grade level, school, district, or state need to analyze the standard and all the indicators that support it, and then create classroom assessments to match the *exact* language of that state standard. For example, *writing a persuasive essay* is a standard that every state requires from second or third grade through high school and college. Yet if a student moves several times, he or she will encounter different indicators, descriptors, components, elements, or benchmarks (depending on the state), which mean essentially the same thing but are phrased differently. For example, one state in the Northeast has standards that say middle school students should produce a persuasive essay that

- Engages the reader by establishing a context, creating a persona, and otherwise developing reader interest;
- Develops a controlling idea that makes a clear and knowledgeable judgment; and
- Creates and organizes a structure that is appropriate to the needs, values, and interests of a specified audience, and arranges details, reasons, examples, and anecdotes effectively and persuasively.

A southern state addresses the same standard by saying middle school students should produce a persuasive essay that

- Engages the reader by establishing a context, creating a speaker's voice, and otherwise developing reader interest;
- States a clear position or perspective in support of a proposition or proposal; and
- Describes the points in support of the proposition, employing well-articulated, relevant evidence.

A midwestern state addresses the same middle school standard by saying that students should write persuasive compositions that

- Establish and develop a controlling idea;
- Support arguments with detailed evidence;
- Exclude irrelevant information; and
- Cite sources of information.

Middle school teachers see the similarities among these different state standards, and they may have to add additional criteria to explain more fully what is required. Some states provide detailed standards and descriptors that spell out every specific requirement, whereas other states provide very broad descriptors that can be interpreted differently. Students may become confused by the terms used and the persuasive writing process described. Effective teachers believe that students need to expand their vocabulary by learning as many synonyms as possible, so it is not unusual to see several terms listed in a checklist showing students what they need to do to complete the assignment.

PERSUASIVE ESSAY CHECKLIST

- Did you write a thesis statement (position or perspective) in support of your proposition (proposal)?
- Did you create a persona (speaker's voice) for the essay?
- Did you employ well-articulated (clear), relevant evidence (facts, statistics, details, reasons, and anecdotes) to persuade your readers?

The language of the standards from one state is not necessarily better than that used in other states, but it is confusing when educational professionals creating state standards sometimes use verbiage that seems designed to daze students—and sometimes their teachers. Some states provide a glossary of terms so that teachers know the definitions and examples. Other states, however,

The language of the standards from one state is not necessarily better than that used in other states, but it is confusing when educational professionals creating state standards sometimes use verbiage that seems designed to daze students—and sometimes their teachers.

provide no glossary of terms or definitions; teachers in these states are forced to interpret the meanings on their own. A set of national standards would require a national vocabulary base that would promote standards-based teaching consistently throughout the United States, as well as help both teachers and students who move out of their states adjust more quickly to the *language of the other state's standards.*

COMMON ASSESSMENTS

Common assessments could be defined as assessments aligned to the power standards identified by the vertical teams of teachers who analyze all the standards across all grade levels. Once these power standards have been identified, the grade-level, department, or vertical teams create some common assessments, such as performance tasks, test bank questions, checklists, or rubrics, that will be assigned to students periodically throughout the school year to assess their understanding and mastery of these important concepts and set specific goals for improvement. According to Ainsworth and Viegut (2006), administrators need to make time throughout the school year to allow teachers to meet collaboratively to score the assessments, analyze the results, and discuss how to use differentiated instructional strategies to help students improve. These interventions are used all through the formative assessment cycle so that students have multiple opportunities to demonstrate their understanding. Ainsworth and Viegut believe that this process of developing and scoring common assessments "informs" instruction as well as offers "predictive value" as to the results students are likely to receive on the large-scale standardized assessments at the end of the year. These collaborative meetings take time, but teachers will begin to realize how their formative classroom assessments fit together with the summative standardized assessments into a cohesive, powerful whole. Ainsworth and Viegut believe, "In glimpsing the potential impact this practice can have on advancing all students to proficiency and beyond, teachers *make time* for this powerful practice" (p. 3, emphasis original).

Schmoker (2002) has found substantial evidence that desirable results are virtually inevitable when teachers work in teams to assess standards. The teams meet to review achievement data and set a limited number of measurable goals. He recommends that teachers focus on one standard such as "measurement" in math and "voice" in writing as a means of targeting specific skills. Schmoker adds that teams should "work regularly and collectively to design, adapt, and assess instructional strategies targeted directly at specific standards of low performance revealed by the assessment data" (p. 11). Language arts teachers in one middle school or from every middle school in the district could meet and assess their students' narrative essays using checklists and rubrics they themselves developed. After examining their students' work, they analyze the data and determine which standards-based terms or processes need more work. They then collaborate and share differentiated strategies to take back to their classrooms to use with the whole class or with individual students who need additional help.

The data are used to determine priority goals, to build collaboration among grade-level or vertical teams of teachers in the same school or district, and to ensure the continuous improvement of the knowledge and skills of all teachers within the community of learners. Figure 5.3 shows a Narrative Writing Checklist developed by a team of fourth- and fifth-grade teachers to guide their students in writing a narrative essay using the language of their state standards.

Stiggins and DuFour (2009) believe, "Common assessments— those created by teams of teachers who teach the same course or grade level—also represent a powerful tool in effective assessment in professional learning communities. Put the two together and the result can redefine the role of assessment in school improvement" (p. 640). When teams of teachers meet regularly to create common assessments and analyze the data to determine next steps, they drive instruction and improve student learning.

EXAMINING STUDENT WORK

One protocol for examining student work developed from the common assessments encourages teachers to use the same rubric to assess all students' work. The same rubric could be used by all students and teachers to achieve greater reliability in their grading. For example, if all students were required to write a persuasive letter to the editor about a topic that concerned them, teachers could create a weighted rubric that listed all the criteria required, as well as a list of descriptors

Standard: Georgia Performance Standard: English/Language Arts 4th Grade, Writing 2 (GPS ELA4W2)

Criteria/Performance Indicators	Not Taught 1	Taught 1
Engages the Reader		
• **Established a context**		
• **Creates a point of view**		
• **Develops reader interest**		
Establishes a Story		
• **Develops plot (fill in the blanks)**		
*Who		
*What		
*Where		
*When		
*Why		
*How		
• **Develops a setting (fill in the blanks)**		
*Where		
*When		
• **Develops conflict (check those that apply)**		
*Man vs. Man		
*Man vs. Nature		
*Man vs. Himself		
*(select other)		
Creates an Organizing Structure		
• **Chronological Order**		
• **Cause and Effect**		
• **Similarity and Differences**		
• **Posing and Answering Questions**		
Uses Sensory Language		
• Uses Descriptive Language		
*Vivid Adjectives		
*Colorful Adverbs		

Criteria/Performance Indicators	Not Taught 1	Taught 1
• Uses Figurative Language		
*Similes		
*Metaphors		
*Personification		
*Onomatopoeia		
Includes Concrete Language		
• Uses action verbs		
• Uses appropriate nouns, pronouns, and descriptions		
Develops Complex Characters		
• Portrays realistic protagonist (main character)		
• Portrays realistic antagonist (foil/bad guy)		
• Uses authentic dialogue		
Utilizes Appropriate Narrative Strategies		
• Uses dialogue to drive plot		
• Establishes tension		
• Interjects suspense		
Provides a Sense of Closure to Writing		
• Foreshadows the ending		
• Builds the story to a climax		
• Develops a *resolution* (explanation at the end)		
• Answers key questions		
• Wraps up loose ends		

Figure 5.3   Task: Narrative Writing Checklist—Fourth Grade

SOURCE: *From Standards to Rubrics in Six Steps: Tools for Assessing Student Learning, K–8* (pp. 49–50), by K. Burke, 2006, Thousand Oaks, CA: Corwin.

that showed evidence of completeness and quality. Figure 5.4 is an example of a common assessment rubric that students use to help guide their efforts and that the teacher uses to provide feedback to help the students improve their work. When the teams of teachers meet to

Standard: Students will be able to write a persuasive letter by using appropriate organization, arguments, information as well as correct usage, conventions, and letter format.

Student Name: _____ Period: _____ Course: _____
Grade: _____

Criteria The student:	1 Do Over!	2 One More Edit!	3 Editor Considers!	4 Editor Publishes!	Score
Purpose of the Letter • Persuade • Call to action • Generate support	Evidence of 1 element	Evidence of 2 elements	Evidence of 3 elements	The letter persuades the reader to agree with author's opinion.	__x6 =__
Organization • Thesis Statement • Support Sentences • Concluding Sentences	Evidence of 1 element	Evidence of 2 elements	Evidence of 3 elements	The organization is logical, coherent, and fluent.	__x5 =__
Arguments • Logical • Factual • Use of Statistics • Use of Quotations	Evidence of 1 element	Evidence of 2 elements	Evidence of 3–4 elements	Arguments use appropriate logic, facts, statistics, and expert quotations to convince readers.	__x6 =__
Letter Format • Date • Inside Address • Salutation • Body • Closing • Signature	Includes 1–2 elements	Includes 3–4 elements	Includes 5–6 elements	The writer follows standards of formal letter writing and capitalizes each and punctuates all elements correctly.	__x4 =__

Criteria The student:	1 Do Over!	2 One More Edit!	3 Editor Considers!	4 Editor Publishes!	Score

Usage
• Complete
  Sentences
• Correct Grammar
• Correct Subject/
  Verb Agreement
	Evidence
	of 1
	element
		Evidence
		of 2
		elements
			Evidence
			of 3
			elements
				Writer
				demonstrates
				correct
				usage and
				uses
				appropriate
				transitions
				for
				coherence.
					__x2 =__

Conventions • Capitalization • Punctuation • Spelling	4 or more errors that damage writer's credibility	2–3 errors that distract from the message	1 error a result of careless proof- reading	Writer uses polished and professional mechanics that editors admire and they publish letter.	__x2 =__

Total Points: _____

(Out of 100)

Scale: 90–100 = A;
      80–89 = B;
      70–79 = C;
Below 69 = Not Yet!

Final Grade: _____

Figure 5.4   Letter to the Editor Weighted Rubric

SOURCE: Adapted from *How to Assess Authentic Learning,* 5th ed., by K. Burke, in press, Thousand Oaks, CA: Corwin. Used with permission.

review student work, they can see quickly what areas of weakness need to be addressed. If many students scored a 1 or a 2 in the section on "Arguments," the teachers discuss how they can implement different strategies to teach the skills more effectively. During this process, teachers also discuss ways of differentiating their instruction in order to meet the needs of their diverse students. Or they may consider ways to revise the rubric to provide more appropriate and precise descriptors if they feel their descriptors are too vague.

The standards-based data that teachers collect from these sessions help them redirect their teaching and assist struggling students who may need interventions. These students would have extra practice and time to improve before they write their summative letter to the editor for their final grade. When teams of teachers examine their students' work, they also analyze the data to predict how their students might perform on a high-stakes assessment that requires them to write a timed persuasive writing piece. The practice helps teachers and students understand the writing and assessment process and build their confidence.

STANDARDS-BASED RUBRICS

Rubrics created by teams of teachers who target the standards and embed the language of the standards in both the criteria and the descriptors provide students and teachers with clear and consistent guidelines. If students know the expectations for quality work *before* they begin a performance task, then they can focus on completing each criterion, as well as improving their work, in order to meet or exceed the standards. Figure 5.5 provides a rubric checklist that helps teachers create rubrics that target the standards and use the vocabulary of the standards as well as all the indicators, benchmarks, competencies, and components within the power standard.

Of course, the data from test scores are important, but the data provided by formative and summative classroom assessments are even more valuable.

Without the common assessments, teachers who meet regularly to examine student work might be comparing apples to oranges if they all gave different assignments and used various methods of assessment. Rubrics included in many textbooks, workbooks, professional development books, or Internet sites may not be valid assessment tools for a specific state. However, rubrics created by teams of teachers who embed the language of the state standards are usually more valid. Teachers who create valid rubrics know that they are preparing their students for both classroom assessments and standardized tests. The Rubric Checklist helps teacher teams create valid teaching rubrics that provide the scaffolding students need to achieve academic success.

Assignment: Self-assess your rubric.	Not Yet 0	Some Evidence 1
Heading:		
• Title of item being assessed ("Rubric for Oral Presentation")		
• State standard/benchmark number and key words (Language Arts Standard 6.5, *"Speaking to persuade"*)		
• Place for student's name, period, course, or grade level		
• Place for date of assessment		
Scoring Levels:		
• Four levels ranging from 1 to 4 (even numbers only)		
• Zero is understood to mean no evidence of effort.		
• The highest score of "4" sets clear expectations of what students must do to exceed standards ("A" work).		
• Scoring levels include number ("1") and description ("Novice").		
• Scoring levels could include pictures that describe levels.		
Descriptors/Elements or Indicators:		
• The umbrella criterion ("Organization") should not be graded; the indented bullet points ("Introduction," "Body") should be graded.		
• The descriptors are concise and specific. (Avoid words/phrases such as "some," "few," "adequate," "good," "most of the time.")		
• The descriptors should use the vocabulary from the state standards as well as synonyms from the textbook.		

(Continued)

(Continued)

Assignment: Self-assess your rubric.	Not Yet 0	Some Evidence 1
• Some criteria can be weighted ("Organization x 4").		
Format:		
• Use graphics and pictures to add visual appeal.		
• Tally each criterion on the side to get a score (Analytical Rubric).		
• Total each criterion score to arrive at a final score.		
• Provide a scale to convert rubric score to final grade.		

Figure 5.5   Rubric Checklist

SOURCE: *From Standards to Rubrics in Six Steps: Tools for Assessing Student Learning, K–8,* by K. Burke, 2006, Thousand Oaks, CA: Corwin. Used with permission.

CONCLUSION

Data play a critical role in driving instruction and assessment in today's standards-based classrooms. Too many educators, however, seem to rely on the data generated from high-stakes standardized tests. Of course, the data from test scores are important, but the data provided by formative and summative classroom assessments are even more valuable. If teacher teams work together to create valid and reliable common assessments correlated to the language of their state standards, they can provide immediate feedback to help all students improve throughout the year. The ongoing interventions that help struggling students, as well as the descriptors to exceed standards that challenge all students, provide the immediate data that drive both instruction and assessment in the standards-based classroom.

REFERENCES

Ainsworth, L., & Viegut, D. (2006). *Common formative assessments: How to connect standards-based instruction and assessment.* Thousand Oaks, CA: Corwin.

Burke, K. (2006). *From standards to rubrics in six steps: Tools for assessing student learning, K–8.* Thousand Oaks, CA: Corwin.

Burke, K. (2009). *How to assess authentic learning* (5th ed.). Thousand Oaks, CA: Corwin.

Burke, K. (In press). *Balanced assessment: From formative to summative.* Bloomington, IN: Solution Tree Press.

DuFour, R. (2004, May). What is a "professional learning community"? *Educational Leadership, 61*(8), 6–11.

Little, J. W., Gearhart, M., Curry, M., & Kafka, J. (2003). Looking at student work for teacher learning, teacher community, and school reform. *Phi Delta Kappan, 85*(3), 185–192.

Reeves, D. B. (2003). *Making standards work: How to implement standards-based assessments in the classroom, school, and district* (3rd ed.). Englewood, CO: Advanced Learning Press.

Schmoker, M. (2001). *The results fieldbook: Practical strategies from dramatically improved schools.* Alexandria, VA: Association for Supervision and Curriculum Development.

Schmoker, M. (2002). Up and away—Lifting low performance. *Journal of Staff Development, 23*(2), 10–13.

Schmoker, M. (2004). Tipping point: From factless reform to substantive instructional improvement. *Phi Delta Kappan, 85*(6), 424–432.

Stiggins, R., & DuFour, R. (2009). Maximizing the power of formative assessments. *Phi Delta Kappan, 90*(9), 640–644.

CHAPTER SIX

DATA

One District's Journey

DOUGLAS OTTO

Data and its manifold uses have become the bedrock for decision making in school districts. Long gone are the days when intuition, experience, or "gut feelings" could guide decisions for teachers, principals, central office administrators, and school board members. Now, high-quality data drive (or should be driving) most decisions that affect school operations. And educators are finding that the use of data is a far more potent resource in convincing constituents of the validity of school district recommendations or decisions. To be successful, however, an extensive mix of information that allows easy access to various kinds of data is imperative.

BACKGROUND

The focus of this chapter is to explain one school district's journey toward more efficient use of data. The Plano Independent School District (ISD) serves 54,000 students in a second-ring suburban community north of Dallas, Texas. As the community has aged, it has rapidly taken on the characteristics of a more urban and mature city. Plano ISD, like most districts, has experienced the transformation from a district operating with a lack of timely data—or even using poor data—to one that demands a wealth of accurate, current, and reliable information. This chapter will explain some of the uses of data that Plano ISD has implemented in order to use its revenues more efficiently, elicit greater student achievement gains, and communicate in a more transparent way with constituents.

The single issue that may have created the most pressing need for relevant, real-time data in most school districts is school reform. Boosting student achievement became the mantra, and districts began clamoring for strategies that produced achievement gains.

The various uses of data have been around for a long time, of course. School districts have used school enrollment projections, building utilization studies, and bus routing, as well as other major operations that relied on the collection and analysis of data. It is ironic that probably the last major area to begin using high-quality data in making decisions is truly the most important operation in any district—that is, the ability to help all students experience success and maximize their potential.

The single issue that may have created the most pressing need for relevant, real-time data in most school districts is school reform. Boosting student achievement became the mantra, and districts began clamoring for strategies that produced achievement gains. Just as important, however, districts perceived the need for databases that yielded information for both program evaluations and individual student performance.

Texas was one of the leading states in the arena of statewide testing. The Texas Accountability System was centered on a testing program that, for the first time, mandated that districts disaggregate their scores by race and socioeconomics. At the same time, Plano was beginning to experience significant demographic changes. Larger numbers of minority and poor students were beginning to move into the district. As superintendent, it became apparent to me and others that the traditional way of doing things was not working for all students. The data did not reveal the true picture of achievement among many student groups.

The Beginning

In the spring of 1996, our district went through a curriculum management audit conducted by University Research Associates. The curriculum management audit is a process based on generally accepted concepts pertaining to effective instruction and curriculum design and delivery. The independent audit examined three data sources: documents, interviews, and site visits.

Although the audit focused on five standards, one of those standards set its sights squarely on data. The standard examined whether the school system used results from system-designed or adopted assessments to adjust, improve, or terminate ineffective practices or programs. In other words, the standard focused on whether or not our district was using data effectively. In fact, one finding in the audit indicated that "use of assessment data for decision making is inadequate." The audit team recommended that the district should "establish and implement a comprehensive, multi-dimensional district assessment program to provide meaningful data for decision making in student learning, program evaluation, and the improvement of teaching."

The curriculum management audit team wrapped up its work that spring; the results were distributed to staff and community during the summer and fall of that same year. This launched our district's quest for better ways to gather, analyze, and use data for decisions surrounding greater productivity in student achievement.

Collaboration and Benchmarking

As Plano ISD was beginning to grapple with the recommendations of the curriculum management audit, our district also embarked on another endeavor that has yielded tremendous benefits with regard to the use of data. Plano was asked to join the Western States Benchmarking Consortium, a small group of school districts representing large, high-performing school systems in the western United States. The districts agreed to meet periodically to engage in dialogue about "best practices" and strategies for improvement, and to share learning from various members' experiences. The consortium, now in its 14th year, includes representatives from the following seven school districts:

- Blue Valley School District, Overland Park, Kansas;
- Cherry Creek School District, Englewood, Colorado;
- Lake Washington School District, Redmond, Washington;
- Peoria Unified School District, Peoria, Arizona;
- Poway Unified School District, Poway, California;
- Vancouver School District, Vancouver, Washington; and
- Plano Independent School District, Plano, Texas.

Superintendents and other staff members from each district meet three times a year to discuss different ways of achieving organizational effectiveness. These effectiveness efforts have been translated into "benchmarks" that articulate the steps toward achieving the highest-quality public education. These statements are intended to assist the districts and individual campuses in recognizing and acting on key areas of emphasis to improve learning for all students.

The consortium has adopted four strategic areas of focus in its benchmarking work. The purpose of identifying these four areas was driven by the belief that targeted efforts in certain broad strategic areas could provide significant leverage in improving student performance. As a result, the consortium benchmark statements are organized in the following four areas: (1) student learning, (2) capacity development, (3) community connectedness, and (4) data-driven decision making.

A total of 16 benchmarks were established to buttress the four strategic areas. Four of the benchmarks support efforts pertaining to data-driven decision making. Supporting each of those four benchmarks are key indicators that are either behavioral or support indicators. *Behavioral indicators* include beliefs or actions that are evident in the system at each level—classroom, campus, and district. *Support indicators* include those factors that support these behaviors, such as professional development, policy, or necessary resources.

The benchmarks and indicators for data-driven decision making include the following:

Using a Variety of Data Effectively

- Relevant Questions and Variables
- Appropriate Information

- Measurement Knowledge and Data Analysis
- Communication
- Data Use
- Institutional Plan for Data Use
- Professional Development
- Data Use in Professional Development

Using Information to Improve Instructional Practice

- Program Evaluation and Planning
- Assessment Strategies
- System Progress Reporting
- Data for Personalization
- Profiling and Monitoring Student Performance
- Alignment Between Data Systems and Standards
- Staff Evaluation Policies
- Instructional Improvement Policy
- Communicating Results
- Professional and Community Development

Using Data to Affect Student Performance

- Belief About the Importance of Data
- Participation in Data Use
- Reliance on Student Performance Data
- Continuous Improvement
- System Support
- System Development
- Data Types
- Data Over Time

Relating Investments, Outcomes, and Improvement Strategies

- Cost/Benefit Analysis
- Data-Informed Decisions
- Integration of Data Systems
- Policy and Procedure
- Professional Development
- Ease of Access and Use of Data

The strategic areas and underlying benchmarks were intended to provide a coherent, connected mechanism for district improvement.

To aid in assessing an organization's development along the continuum of improvement as it related to each of the strategic areas, benchmarks, and indicators, the consortium identified four stages of development. These stages of development could be used at either the district or the local building level.

The four stages of development included the following:

Emergent. This stage describes a school system that is beginning to recognize the need for change in a strategic area. There is increasing discussion of this need, but system leaders have not yet decided what actions to take to bring about the change. There are frequent debates about the advisability of the change, and district policy frequently offers no guidance regarding the possible nature of the change.

Islands. This stage describes a school system that has some "pockets" of change underway. These initiatives have grown out of a certain level of discomfort with current practices in some settings. The discomfort is not yet systemic, and the pilot change efforts often tend to emerge from the bottom up within the system. Such early change efforts tend to be isolated from each other, but are beginning to be the subject of broader debate and attention at the policy and central-office levels regarding their effects and possible consequences for the system.

Integrated. This stage describes a school system that has formally decided on and is integrating significant strategic changes across the entire system—moving from isolated to systemic changes in policy, management, and instructional practices. The system generally operates from the best of what we know about highly effective organizations. Such systems are widely recognized as leaders in strategic improvement and are even called on for advice in shaping state policy. While the system's strategic improvements are well defined and carefully implemented, a district at this stage continues to focus on making the changes truly pervasive across the system, including engendering strong understanding, support, and collaboration from the broader community.

Exemplary. This stage describes a school system that demonstrates unusually high levels of student and organizational performance. It is constantly "pushing the envelope"—continuously learning from its data and experience, never totally satisfied with current levels of organizational effectiveness. The system also monitors future trends within and outside the community to determine where new policies and practices (and paradigms) might be needed down the road. It expends considerable efforts in planning for these adjustments. Some might call this level "world class" in that such exemplary practices are attainable, but unmatched by most other educational systems around the world. Moreover, because it is recognized for its accomplishments, a district at this level often leads broader efforts in improving quality of life for children, youth, and families, both within and outside its local community.

The benchmarks may be used throughout various levels of school organizations. For example, the superintendent, cabinet, and board members might place initial focus on performing a pre-assessment of the district's current status. In addition, district administrative departments may assess their effectiveness and progress toward improvement by using the self-assessment. Schools, also, within the framework of the school-based improvement process, may find the self-assessment valuable.

Members of the Western States Benchmarking Consortium expect and encourage a wide variety of uses of the benchmarks. For example, districts and individual campuses may choose to use the statements in the following ways:

- As a template for reviewing and renewing school improvement plans;
- As a way to identify new priorities for improvement;
- As a means to deepen the shared vision of "quality" across the system; or
- As a template to help individual school campuses assess progress.

The seven member districts also inserted some helpful techniques in order to make the benchmarks more user-friendly. First, each benchmark under the strategic area of data-driven decision making includes an "impact question." The purpose of the impact question is to frame the

Each benchmark indicator includes a "guiding question" that allows educators to think about the indicator from the same reference point. These guiding questions frame discussion of each indicator.

discussion for educators as they begin to examine each of the indicators that are attached to the benchmarks. In turn, each indicator includes a "guiding question" that allows educators to think about the indicator from the same reference point. For example, one indicator under the benchmark of "using a variety of data effectively" deals with measurement knowledge and data analysis. The guiding question asks, "What is the evidence that key decision makers have the knowledge/skills to collect, analyze, and use different kinds of data for improvement planning?" So this guiding question now frames discussion around the indicator.

In addition, each indicator under the benchmarks also includes "possible evidence" that the district is addressing that particular indicator. For example, using the same indicator mentioned in the paragraph above, some possible evidence that the campus or district is addressing measurement knowledge and data analysis would be evidence of systematic training and assessment literacy provided to all decision makers. Other possible examples of evidence might be campuses and departments identifying and using their own data to augment district data, or school/department improvement plans displaying multiple measures and multiple forms of analysis.

The importance of the benchmarks cannot be overstated. The benchmark document, which has now been used for more than a decade, has provided guidance to Western States Benchmarking Consortium districts and other reform-minded districts that have used the benchmarks. While this chapter concerns itself only with those benchmarks that pertain to data, other benchmarks exist for the other three strategic areas: student achievement, building district capacity, and community connections. The benchmark document is in the public domain and can be accessed at www.wsbenchmark.org.

CURRICULUM MANAGEMENT AND ASSESSMENT SYSTEMS

The Plano Independent School District has used a variety of dedicated student assessment and accountability data systems since the mid-1990s. The earliest attempts at providing student data for use within the schools consisted of spreadsheets forwarded to each campus principal as results became available from state testing or such nationally normed tests as the Iowa Tests of Basic Skills (ITBS). These results were often reported up to 6 months after the tests were administered; the usefulness of the data in bringing about changes in student instruction was minimal. Teachers who did not receive the test results until the end of the year were obviously unable to use the information to intervene on behalf of students.

Our first attempt at centralizing student assessment information on a districtwide database came in 1997 with the adoption of an off-the-shelf software program. The use of this system required a central database coupled with a client software program that had to be installed on every computer that accessed the central database. This method was designed to eliminate the need to provide spreadsheets to each campus, but this early networked software database was not up to the task of supporting real-time access with 100 percent reliability. As a result, spreadsheets still had to be created and disseminated. The need to install a client software package on each classroom computer was also a significant support issue, with nearly 4,000 teacher computers in use at the time.

This software solution promised to deliver student assessment information to each teacher's desktop. That promise was achieved, but the system was still unable to provide results quickly. A client-server software solution, such as the one Plano ISD was using, ultimately proved to be too much of a support challenge, since each computer needed the client software (and associated updates) installed individually.

In 2000–2001, the district began to evaluate Web-based assessment software that would eliminate the need to individually install software on each teacher's computer. Instead, the district felt the need to rely on a standard Web browser application. It was determined that a different solution than what was already in use best met the needs of the district.

As a Web-based software package, this newly selected solution allowed updates to occur only on the Web server, which meant that the browser on each teacher's computer could make use of new enhancements immediately. However, as was the case with every early Web-based database software package, this solution did not allow teachers to ask their own questions and find the answers through their use of the data. In other words, each report needed to be designed and coded individually. In addition, this Web-based system continued to support only "autopsy style" reports, since data returned from state tests and the ITBS still required months of processing before they could be added to the database. In addition, as teachers and principals provided ideas for new reports, the list of available reports generated by the system quickly grew to over 600.

At this time, a new series of obstacles to effective data use began to emerge. Selecting reports from such an enormous list became burdensome, and teachers reverted to using primarily the simplest reports to gain information (after the fact) about their students. Printing from Web-based software also lacked the sophistication that many staff members requested when hard copies were required. So once again, the district found itself trying to make use of a third-party vendor software system that lacked the flexibility to provide teachers with the information that they needed most. In addition, the sheer number of available reports generated by the system was simply too overwhelming.

In 2003–2004, the entire Plano ISD began using a new local achievement measurement produced by the Northwest Evaluation Association, called the Measures of Academic Progress (MAP). This computerized adaptive test took the place of all other nationally normed assessments (such as the ITBS) and made it possible for teachers to have results within 24 hours. At the same time, the limitations of the existing Web-based software data system were delaying the efforts of the district to move beyond autopsy-style results and enter into the arena of predictive modeling. Adaptive tests are more accurate due to the fact that the next question presented to a student is predicated on the correct or incorrect answer to the previous question.

After reviewing a number of proprietary student assessment and business intelligence solutions during the spring of 2004, Plano ISD determined that the Enterprise Intelligence Suite, from SAS Institute, Inc., provided the best match with the district's current and projected needs. The goal for the new assessment system was to provide teachers and principals with predictive information on likely student performance in upcoming assessments, so as to allow interventions to be made early in the school year that could positively affect student performance on state assessments administered in the spring.

The goal for the new assessment system was to provide teachers and principals with predictive information on likely student performance in upcoming assessments, so as to allow interventions to be made early in the school year.

The analytical and modeling tools available in SAS allowed new methods of combining multiple variables to be run against student assessment information in near real-time fashion. Combining results from state assessments, ability assessments (CogAT), and adaptive achievement assessments (MAP) to provide expected student results was now possible. In addition, having the system identify specific areas of improvement to positively affect those expected results is not available through typical educational assessment software tools.

The advanced statistical capabilities provided by SAS have provided a new lens through which student achievement is viewed districtwide. The primary example is the expected student growth chart derived for each of the 54,000-plus students through the use of SAS analytical models and a performance management portal. The portal is the Web site that parents go to for information about their child's achievement (see further below). These achievement results are based on the use of the SAS analytical models. This growth chart is available for teacher and student use at all times and has been recently introduced for parent use through their portal into the district Web site. In addition, teachers have the ability to ask their own questions of the data. This gives a more complete view of individual student achievement.

ADVANCED USE OF ASSESSMENT SYSTEMS

With a new performance management system using advanced analytical procedures in place, Plano ISD has now determined how to measure students' academic growth within a framework that mitigates many of the arguments teachers, administrators, and community members have made against other existing accountability or growth models. Plano ISD's model measures growth in a way that is fair to all students, regardless of ability; fair to all teachers, regardless of the diversity of students assigned to them; and fair to all campuses, regardless of their concentrations of diverse populations, including special-needs students, students from low-income families, and those with limited English proficiency (LEP).

As indicated, an important attribute of Plano ISD's growth model is that it is fair to all teachers and campuses in relation to the amount of growth expected of each student. As district leaders researched the growth or value-added models currently in existence, we learned that these models often do not take into consideration that children's cognitive starting point has a significant effect on their gains measured at the end of an academic time period. Therefore, as an important component in Plano's growth model, we use Riverside Publishing's CogAT measure to determine the cognitive composition of teachers' classes and the enrollment of a school building. These cognitive measures are included in the growth models, along with state assessment measures and MAP measures. In addition, LEP status, special education status, and other demographic variables are used to chart the expected rate of growth for like groups of students within classrooms and campuses. As a result, one teacher's group of students or one building's students do not have an advantage of reaching academic growth expectations more easily compared to another group or building due to those differences in students that may not be within teacher or campus control.

The Plano ISD growth model not only provides a measure of improvement but is also useful to the district in isolating the effect on student performance of programs, interventions, and teachers. The growth model allows the district to quantify performance in terms of months of instruction. This metric enables the district to evaluate the effectiveness of programs in terms of time versus rate of learning, and thereby identify the most effective educational practices.

THE PARENT PORTAL

An important component of effective data use is the ability of information to be accessed by all stakeholders. In a school district, that means that students and parents should have ready access to information that affects student achievement.

In Plano ISD, students and parents have access to this type of information through their individual Web-based portals called myPISD.net. Each of the 54,000 students has his or her own unique network account; the portal is presented directly to them as they log in to the network each day.

In addition, parents and guardians have their own portal accounts and have access to the learning resources available to their children, as well as real-time grades, attendance data, and assessment information. This includes easy-to-understand visuals such as

Do	Don't
Identify and create an inventory of data elements to be collected.	Collect and store data simply because they're available.
Include teachers, counselors, and administrators in identifying necessary data elements.	Create data element lists in isolation.
Set a goal to have information readily available to every stakeholder.	Attempt to deliver universal access in the first phase of your implementation.
Consider multiple measures when evaluating student achievement.	Rely on a state assessment measure as the only view of student performance.
Provide data capture processes that ensure data integrity.	Assume that the data in your existing systems are accurate.
Provide ongoing professional development to teachers, administrators, and parents in the use of student data.	Provide data reports without ensuring proper understanding of the report and its appropriate uses.
Identify clearly which questions you want to answer and what data provide insight into those questions.	Use data haphazardly to answer questions that were not designed to be answered with those data.

Table 6.1   Dos and Don'ts

the expected achievement growth charts for all students. The parent portal is available through any Internet-connected device, including cell phones.

DATA USES BEYOND STUDENT ACHIEVEMENT

In addition to the innovative use of business intelligence tools to support more effective use of student achievement data, Plano ISD has been involved in developing a new student/finance/human resource accounting system, using an open framework structure and running on a single database since 2003. That development has now reached its final stages, with only a few financial modules yet to be fully implemented. This significant achievement has provided decision makers with highly reliable and accessible data to inform daily decisions. The use of a single database for these important school business functions provides for a higher level of data integrity than the district has ever had, and allows seamless integration with other data systems, such as the student assessment portal.

The final goal of the district's data information structure is now within reach. The ability to combine all data variables that have an impact on student achievement is possible due to the design of these databases and the software tools used to analyze and display results.

The Challenge

It could be said that the most useful definition of the term *data-enhanced decision making* is getting the right data, to the right person, at the right time, in the right format. The challenge, of course, is getting all four parts of the equation correct. The best place to start is at the beginning. Educators need to ask themselves what information they really need in order to help make appropriate decisions regarding allocation of resources, staffing, student achievement, and every other issue that requires data to make an informed decision. So those questions regarding what kinds of data are needed are just as important as the databases that must be constructed to provide the information. Giving direction and focus to the right questions will yield the best data and the most effective use of data.

> It could be said that the most useful definition of the term data-enhanced decision making *is getting the right data, to the right person, at the right time, in the right format. The challenge, of course, is getting all four parts of the equation correct.*

Finally, in concert with asking the right questions, districts must ensure that they have the right policies in place to allow for the collection, dissemination, and uses of information. As policies help communicate and provide direction to a district's mission and vision, they should also address the district's philosophy and practices regarding how data are collected and used.

CHAPTER SEVEN

INFORMATION AND COMMUNICATIONS TECHNOLOGY IN EDUCATION

JESSE RODRIGUEZ

The future holds that effective learning will require that information be available anytime, anywhere. This, in turn, will force educational institutions to give serious thought to how future acquisitions of technology will make possible the interaction and free flow of information among students, educators, parents, the local community, and, increasingly, the global community. Inherent in all of this will be the need for a communications infrastructure that will allow all manner of devices to tap into information resources in a variety of ways, i.e., inter- and intranets, satellite, cable, and wireless.

This chapter will *not* provide an in-depth analysis of the benefits of anytime, anywhere learning. Instead, it assumes that one-to-one computing, regardless of the technology used, is a desired, and desirable, outcome. It will address the issues associated with implementing an information network capable of supporting this outcome. The key concepts addressed in this chapter are important for organization-wide effective implementation of technology.

It should be clear herein that the relationship between the district superintendent and the chief information officer (CIO) of the district is central to how well an educational institution addresses the critical issues involved in implementing technology effectively. This is natural, given the importance of technology to education and the impact that decisions made in this arena will have on the instructional, budgetary, and governance realms of every school district. It is imperative that superintendents be able to place the utmost trust in their CIOs. Like the superintendent, the CIO is one of the few administrators in any school system who has responsibilities bridging the administrative and instructional arenas. To illustrate this, let's look at the critical issues facing schools today and, from that vantage point, extrapolate the importance of the relationship between superintendent and CIO, and how critical it is that they work together as a team.

GETTING STARTED

Several challenges must be addressed in order to ensure that successful information and communications technology (ICT) systems capable of supporting the school district's initiatives can be implemented. They are as follows:

First, what technologies will be purchased and used?

Second, how will the curriculum and technology be integrated?

Third, what safeguards will be needed to ensure appropriate access to information?

Finally, there are a number of ancillary issues that will have an impact on the successful implementation of technology.

These four broad issues are closely intertwined; how one approaches and resolves any one of them will have repercussions for the other three.

WHAT TECHNOLOGIES WILL BE PURCHASED AND USED?

In a most fundamental way, this first issue is the toughest decision school leaders will need to make. This decision will have the greatest impact on teaching and learning and on the organization in terms of allocation of resources and long-term relevance in an increasingly digital world.

Simply stated, leaders must decide how central technology will be to the organization—both instructionally and administratively.

Simply stated, leaders must decide how central technology will be to the organization—both instructionally and administratively. When we look at the world around us, we see significant shifts in progress; most forms of communication and information flow are rapidly becoming digital in nature.

One of the most important processes that a school system can undertake is to develop a cohesive plan for the implementation of technology. The emphasis of any plan should be on what an organization wants to accomplish, not on how it will accomplish it. Organizations should look to acquiring technology not as a means of creating a specialized program—such as a notebook program, in which each student uses a laptop computer to replace textbooks for a good portion of the curriculum, for instance—but as a way of making the organization more efficient and as a means of adding value to both internal and external constituencies. In the case of a notebook program, the value added would come in providing content anytime and anywhere for the student. Were a notebook program tied into an organization's content-management system, for example, an additional value would be added by allowing the student, the school, and the parent access to information detailing the progress of the student and also by providing access to additional content tied to areas in which the student needs assistance. Strategies for the acquisition of technology should indeed be strategic, not tactical, as a means of providing high-value services and staying adaptable to constantly changing needs. Each technology purchase should be viewed with some thought as to its potential use outside of the immediate purpose for its purchase.

The logical next step is to determine how technology can assist in accomplishing the stated goals of the school system. Integral to this step is the development of a feedback mechanism designed to measure the effectiveness of any given technology initiative and allow for changes to take place to accommodate new requirements as they develop. In addition, to bring order and structure to the organization, the plan should provide for the institutionalization of common business practices and funding support. From the standpoint of technology, there can be no more important set of business practices than those dealing with the setting of standards to assist an organization in achieving economies of scale and implementing relevant support mechanisms.

The other side of the technology issues coin is personnel issues. Even the best technology plan is only as good as the personnel tasked with designing, building, supporting, and maintaining complex information systems. How well an organization has planned for the recruitment, retention, and certification of its information systems personnel—or the outsourcing of these services—will determine the success of its technology program.

The following questions need to be asked:

- How does this purchase or program fit into the overall goals of the organization?
- Will the technology represent an evolution of what is already in place, or will it require drastic new competencies of staff members? What are the budgetary implications?
- Is the technology adaptable? To the best of our ability to foresee the future, will this technology have staying power, or will it need to be replaced as new standards emerge? Should we implement now or wait?

Probably the most important change that school systems must accept is that they need to view technology as core to the organization's ability to function. School systems to date have, by and large, not looked to the regular capital or maintenance and operations funds as a means of funding technology. Much of the technology purchases are done through one-time or uncertain sources of money such as bonds; budget overrides; and grants or donations, be they governmental, private, or corporate. What makes this process so tenuous is that, increasingly, the organization's ability to survive and thrive will depend on its ability to gather, manage, and communicate information well.

Define the Infrastructure

All too often, long drawn-out battles are fought over the types of equipment that will end up on the desktop, without a great deal of thought being given to the communication infrastructure necessary to make technology viable. *Infrastructure* is defined here as the communication network composed of wiring, wiring patch panels, and communication rooms to which all computer equipment (i.e., servers, PCs, routers, switches) will connect.

It cannot be overemphasized how important it is for educational institutions to establish a stable infrastructure for information systems. Planned and implemented correctly, infrastructure should last 20 or more years. It seems increasingly likely that needed information is likely to reside somewhere else rather than on a specific device—be it a desktop, laptop, or handheld device that an individual is using. Access to information is the key concept here, and it should be understood that this information is likely to exist somewhere other than on the device a student or school employee uses on a day-to-day basis. The information might exist on a server at the school, at the school headquarters—or even somewhere across the world, for that matter. It might exist in a format that is not normally compatible with the device being used, such as a Smartphone, for instance.

The real value to any organization is in the exchange of data and information, and in having a digital "highway" robust enough to handle the exchange of information, whether it be data, voice, or video. Having systems able to access this information, format it for use in the device making the request for information; tying the use of the information to curricular or administrative initiatives; and, finally, being able to use this information to allow programmatic changes to take place within the organization and to report this information to interested constituencies such as parents—these will be key to the continuing success of any organization.

Establish Process Standards

A criticism made of acquisitions of both educational and administrative technology has been the poor return on what is often a considerable investment. The challenge for schools will be to develop standards that ensure that the organization can acquire appropriate technology at the best possible prices—technology that can be economically supported and maintained—while at the same time providing sufficient flexibility to meet the individual needs of schools and departments. Let me emphasize strongly that what I am proposing here is not buying equipment with only the lowest possible price in mind, but rather looking at any acquisition from the perspective of the total cost of ownership over the useful life of the purchase.

Institute Effective Personnel
Practices to Retain Key Personnel

From a technology standpoint, it is important to ask, what good is good technology without competent personnel to support it? The dichotomy facing organizations today is that as technology becomes easier to use, it is, at the same time, becoming much more complex to implement and maintain. This difficulty will become even more pronounced as school systems continue to acquire more and more technology, especially in the areas of accountability and reporting. Highly qualified individuals will be needed to run these complex systems, even considering the recommendation made later in this chapter to buy equipment and software with "smarts" built in. The school organization must develop a plan to retain those individuals who are doing a good job. One way to do this is to provide funding that will allow these individuals to gain or keep certification in their respective fields. (By the way, it costs an organization less to keep a qualified individual over the long term than it does to hire and train replacements.) Outsourcing will continue to be necessary; this is addressed in the Ancillary Issues section of this chapter.

The dichotomy facing organizations today is that as technology becomes easier to use, it is, at the same time, becoming much more complex to implement and maintain. This difficulty will become even more pronounced.

To summarize, a good plan will deal with the following:

- Separating the "what" from the "how" and the "who" in developing a plan:
    - *What* is to be accomplished?
    - *How* can technology assist in accomplishing the stated goals?
    - *How* will success be measured?

- ○ *Who* is responsible for providing direction?
- ○ *Who* sets hardware standards? Software standards?
- Define the infrastructure.
- Ensure equity across the organization.
- Ensure that all equipment is digital, not analog, in nature. Wherever possible, integrate telephony, video, and data equipment.
- Use "intelligent" switching equipment instead of "dumb" hubs to connect users to the network.
- Standardize hardware and software configurations.
- Purchase hardware and software with built-in intelligent manageability.
- Ensure that back-end equipment has fault-tolerant features.
- Establish process standards:
  - ○ Standardization versus individual initiative
  - ○ Hardware
  - ○ Software

How Will Technology Be Acquired and Kept Relevant Over Time?

Another major issue facing school systems is how to keep the technology relevant. The current strategy for most organizations is to purchase the needed technology outright. The problem with this strategy is that, after just a few years, there is little to show for the expenditures. Computer equipment rapidly becomes obsolete, and later purchases often do not mesh well with that which is already in place. Support of the technology infrastructure thus becomes not only more difficult but also more expensive.

While procurement rules often make it impossible for schools to lease technology, administrators should give serious thought to working with both key internal constituencies and outside agencies to change this mind-set and, where necessary, the rules and regulations that prevent leasing. Consideration should be given to standardizing by using specific vendors, where it is possible and makes sense, for the different types of computer equipment needed by the organization. Requests for proposals (RFPs) and requests for information (RFIs) and bids would specify a brand and model, but the process would still be competitive, as different vendors and their resellers would be able to bid on the lowest price to deliver specified equipment.

THE ADVANTAGES OF LEASING

The leasing of technology provides several distinct advantages. First, it allows an organization to purchase more equipment up front. Assume, for example, that a school system has a plan to place needed technology across all its sites over a 3-year period. With leasing, the organization would purchase, during the first year, all the equipment slated for purchase over a 3-year period. Pricing will be better since the organization can negotiate a better price per computer based on a larger number of computers being purchased at one time. Moreover, such a strategy would deal up front with the issue of equity by ensuring that all schools would receive new computer equipment at the same time. This would go a long way toward making hardware and software support easier, since staff would only have to support one type of computer with the same capabilities across the entire organization, as opposed to the current practice in many school systems of trying to support a broad spectrum of computer types, makes, and models, each with different capabilities.

Leasing also allows the organization to plan for the replacement of its technology infrastructure. In these times of ever-shrinking school budgets, technology has become essential in an organization's day-to-day operations as a means of realizing efficiency, automation, and cost containment. Leasing provides the mechanism for institutionalizing the need to stay technologically relevant by providing for the planned replacement of technology and addressing the ever-increasing rapidity of equipment obsolescence. In the old days, equipment could be migrated down from high schools to middle schools and from middle schools on down to elementary schools. Back then, computer hardware was more capable than the software designed to run on it. This is no longer the case.

Equity is also a pressing concern today. Parents today look to schools to provide appropriate equipment at all grade levels. This will become even more prevalent as the melding of voice, video, and data continues to accelerate.

Clearly, these trends will have an impact not only on computers but also on the purchase of servers, switches, and routers to which these computers connect. Leasing addresses these issues.

Finally, a lease allows services to be bundled. Maintenance contracts, for instance, can be made a part of the lease. With large purchases of equipment, the organization can negotiate favorable terms on such contracts by requiring and receiving better pricing on maintenance than is true with the standard maintenance charges imposed by computer manufacturers and other service providers, which determine their pricing as if the organization were buying only one computer and taking out maintenance on that lone computer. Moreover, as lean as most organizations today are forced to be in the hiring of technical staff, hardware and software setups can be made a part of the lease, as well as the removal of equipment at the end of the lease. All of these are costs that an organization must bear, but which are rarely factored in at the time that computer equipment is acquired.

To summarize its advantages, leasing

- Allows an organization to purchase equipment up front.
- Allows an organization to plan for replacement of technology.
- Addresses the rapid obsolescence of equipment.
- Deals with the limited ability to cascade equipment downward.
- Allows an organization to bundle services.
- Incorporates maintenance contracts.
- Provides for removal of equipment at end of the lease.
- Covers hardware and software setups.

STANDARDIZATION OF EQUIPMENT

Integral to the idea of leasing is the concept of standardizing the equipment to be purchased. Standardization offers several distinct advantages. The current strategy of all too many school districts is to acquire technology and related services based on the lowest bid. The appropriate strategy *should* be to look at the total cost of ownership of any purchase of equipment and services—not just at the purchase price. An alternative approach would be to select a manufacturer of equipment based on criteria beneficial to the organization. Once those criteria have been decided, the

The current strategy of all too many school districts is to acquire technology and related services based on the lowest bid. The appropriate strategy should be to look at the total cost of ownership of any purchase of equipment and services—not just at the purchase price.

selection of a dealer to provide the needed equipment can be made through the bidding process, with the award going to the dealer providing the best pricing for the equipment and services required.

Another advantage, alluded to in the leasing section, is that it will prove to be less costly for the organization to support the equipment of one manufacturer than to try to support equipment from multiple manufacturers. Moreover, staff members need only acquire functional expertise on the products of a single computer manufacturer.

Finally, by standardizing, the organization can lay the foundation for a structured approach to building its information systems infrastructure. Future purchases can be made with a high degree of confidence that they will mesh well with previous purchases. This also lends itself to a potentially fruitful relationship with the equipment manufacturer. Over time, the organization can benefit from additional services, such as access to the long-term strategic plans of the manufacturer, as well as potentially play a role in the future development of products.

Standardize Hardware and Software Steps

Historically, training and support is an area that most school systems have not funded adequately. Three strategies should be undertaken to address this deficiency:

1. As emphasized in this chapter, the organization should standardize the hardware and software it uses, giving particular attention to developing standard configurations based on the equipment being acquired.

2. The organization should acquire and use a systematized "help desk" that interfaces with the organization's other hardware and software management systems as a means of providing support to end-users as issues with hardware and software applications arise. When such a help desk is integrated with other districtwide systems, the organization can develop a database of common solutions; the system can also be a means of receiving feedback on the support being provided.

3. The organization should look to acquiring technology that will enable it to reduce total cost of ownership as it goes about providing training and support.

Having the same hardware configurations across the organization means that the school system can employ tools and strategies not possible with myriad equipment from different manufacturers. The same holds true for software. It becomes much easier (and less expensive) to support application software if the same software is installed across all machines districtwide. Having the same versions and patches on all computers makes it easier for support staff to troubleshoot problems. It also helps to reduce the amount of courses needed to train staff. For example, if there are two different versions of Microsoft Word in use by the organization, two training sessions are necessary to support users of each version. In addition, the exchange of information becomes more difficult to accomplish.

One final thought: There should be no distinction between administrative and instructional networks—it's all bits and bytes. How information is used within the organization might differ, but keep in mind that it's still the same information.

HOW WILL CURRICULUM AND TECHNOLOGY BE INTEGRATED?

This question has proved itself a great conundrum to education. Certainly, part of the answer is that education must come to depend on technology as a key component in the educational process. Sadly, today this is not the case. Schools tend to acquire technology and technology systems on a case-by-case basis—to meet a specific need for a specific department, for example. Little thought is given to how a new system will fit with what is already in place or how this purchase is likely to affect future acquisitions. From a funding standpoint, few organizations target general funds for the acquisition of technology, relying instead on grants or other outside sources of money, thus making for an uncertain future. Few educational organizations have instituted programs that take a long-term look at the acquisition, maintenance, and integration of technology systems; even fewer consider how technology can bring efficiencies of scale or improve the process of teaching and learning. Contrast this with other industries in which technology is a key part of making companies competitive and adaptable.

Put another way, school systems will need to get to a place where, if the information systems aren't functioning properly, education will simply not be possible. To reach that point will require that staff be sufficiently trained and assisted by a support infrastructure. There will also be a need for much more equipment aimed at allowing the organization to depend more on technology as a means of delivering content to students. Finally, schools will need to move away from an environment in which the teacher is the primary provider of information to one in which the student takes on that primary role, with the teacher acting as guide and mentor.

Along the way, schools will need to take the following steps to ensure a successful transition:

Look to the Web for Content. There should be someone in the organization tasked with finding the appropriate resources to redefine the curriculum so that cognitive content and technology mastery objectives are provided in a seamless and thematically integrated series of curriculum units. It is important to note that where most technology programs fail is in not providing teachers with appropriate and related instructional material.

Look to Technology to Assist in Training and Support. As the organization's information systems become more pervasive and complex, the organization should look to technology to assist in providing timely support in the most cost-effective manner possible. For example, support systems exist today that allow hardware or software support to be done remotely; support staff can provide immediate support, and end-users need not wait hours (or days) before getting assistance. Some systems, such as HP OpenView, can even provide preventive maintenance so that failing components are logged and can be replaced before they fail. New versions of software, such as Microsoft Office, can repair themselves should key modules become damaged or accidentally deleted.

To summarize, to develop a good training and support infrastructure, consider the following:

- Standardize hardware and software.
- Standardize desktop configurations.
- Implement a help desk.
- Develop a database of common solutions.
- Create a feedback mechanism.
- Look to technology to assist in training and support.

WHAT SAFEGUARDS WILL BE NEEDED
TO ENSURE APPROPRIATE ACCESS TO INFORMATION?

School systems, as is true of so many other organizations, are relying more on information that is stored in electronic form. This trend will only accelerate as more technology is introduced into the organization at every level. As more computers come online, the ability to restrict access to information will become more difficult. In addition, online sources will often be the only place where one can go to obtain needed information. Therefore, it is important to be aware that the security of information will become a paramount concern. Security of information, as defined here, comes in two forms: physical and logical.

As more computers come online, the ability to restrict access to information will become more difficult. In addition, online sources will often be the only place where one can go to obtain needed information.

The organization should evaluate the need to acquire hardware that has built-in fault-tolerance capabilities. *Fault tolerance* simply means that the failure of any one component should not mean the loss of information that might be irreplaceable. Fault-tolerant equipment is more expensive, unfortunately. The additional cost, however, should be balanced against its value to the organization. The organization must ask itself, what are our data worth? The purchase of fault-tolerant equipment should be viewed in the same way as the purchase of an insurance policy: It is often painful to pay the premium, but sometimes it comes in handy. Fault-tolerant hardware should also allow for remote monitoring and support, as discussed in the previous section in the area of training and support.

The other side to security is more difficult to comprehend, but no less important: the logical safeguarding of electronically stored information. At certain times, people will have legitimate need to access information. Steps must be taken to ensure that access to information occurs in a deliberate, protected manner. For example, what happens when an individual moves from one site to another or into another position within the district? Also, as schools begin to make the transition to becoming value-added, self-service organizations, in which services and content are geared toward the individual instead of a group, serious consideration will need to be given to what sort of services will be made available to students, staff, and the community at large. Parents are beginning to request online access to student information, especially data on their children. Ensuring the appropriate release of information will become vitally important to the organization and should be taken into account as systems are developed and put in place.

Certainly, using software programs that are designed to work together will reduce the chance that something will go wrong. Such software needs to be networkable, as information is likely to reside anywhere on the organization's network. The tighter the integration of the software being used, the easier the process will be to manage. The goal should be to simplify wherever possible. Finally, where appropriate, it should be the stated goal of the organization to purchase software that is database-aware, so that as schools acquire content- and curriculum-management systems and develop data repositories and data warehouses, data can flow easily across the entire organization.

Consideration needs to be given to hiring a database administrator to assist in establishing processes and procedures that take into account the dynamic nature of the organization. This individual should also assist in developing policies related to the accessing and use of information inside and outside the organization's network.

Information flow must constantly be reevaluated to make sure that it empowers rather than hobbles operations. Ours is no longer an industrial society; it is an information society. It is important to understand and accept that change will be constant and ongoing. Organizations must plan for this.

To summarize, in order to ensure the security of the organization's electronically stored information, consider the following:

- Acquire hardware that
  - Has built-in fault-tolerance components.
  - Can be monitored and managed remotely.
- Acquire software that
  - Is integrated.
  - Is networkable.
  - Is database-aware.
- Hire a database administrator.
- Simplify! Reduce complexity wherever possible.

ANCILLARY ISSUES

Consider the following guidelines for instituting selective processes that will allow for a sustainable, adaptable technology infrastructure.

Outsourcing

Outsourcing, in broad terms, is the purchase of services that originally were done in-house. Organizations are increasingly turning to outsourcing but don't seem to understand the issues that must be addressed when entering into such agreements. This section seeks to provide practical guidance and advice in this area.

To begin with, the organization should have specific business objectives that lead to any decision to outsource services. These should be identified and confirmed in the work undertaken during an analysis phase, and prior to selecting a preferred outsourcing services supplier. With those tasks completed, the major objective remaining is to negotiate a supply agreement with the preferred outsourcer for the delivery of the required services at an agreed-upon cost and level of performance. There are six components to an agreement that achieves this objective:

1. **Service specification.** Set out in specific and measurable terms the services required, how they are to be delivered, and the duration for which they are required.

2. **Service levels.** Set the performance standards (service levels) that relate to each of the services to be provided.

3. **Roles and responsibilities.** Document the obligations of the outsourcer and the purchaser and the boundaries of responsibility.

4. **Transition period and acceptance.** Specify how any existing services will be handed over to the outsourcer and the services accepted by the purchaser.

5. **Prices, payment, and duration.** Draw up an agreement on the price and payment for delivery of the services, including the basis of charging for any additional or optional services.

6. **Agreement administration.** Specify how the agreement will be managed and administered, including provision for resolving disputes and the remedies in the event of non-performance.

Develop a Feedback System for Continuous Improvement

Information systems are not static. If they are to remain viable for the organization, they will need to change and adapt over time. The implementation of the following steps will assist administrators in constructing an information system that is continuously adaptable.

First, analyze and understand the organization's flow of information. To ensure that the organization can build an information system that can adapt over time and meet the information needs of the organization, it will need to implement a program to continuously analyze and understand the organization's information flow. This process must center itself on four key questions:

1. Where are the data coming from?
2. Who is using them?
3. What are the people who receive the data doing with them?
4. Should they be receiving them?

Evaluate and redirect the information flow to improve efficiency. This process will be dynamic, ebbing and flowing as data are evaluated and the information flow is redirected to improve efficiency. Information should be generated for a single reason: to assist management and staff in attaining stated goals. If the goal is to improve student test scores, then one must evaluate data coming in to document success and failure and to identify potential problem areas. Also, tools must be developed that will point to what works, what doesn't work, and why.

Establish an organizational biofeedback system. It is important to place collection points throughout the organization to create a biofeedback system. Such a system should be constructed as part of an ongoing process—not as a separate and stand-alone system. A help desk is a perfect example of a biofeedback system.

Use office automation as a facilitator of information system strategy. Office automation must be used as a tool to move information throughout the organization. The organization must ensure that applications are database-aware and use tools that will facilitate the exchange and management of information, i.e., document management software or groupware software that allows for collaboration.

To summarize, the organization should do the following when building a system that will continuously improve:

- Analyze and understand the organization's flow.
- Define up front what is to be monitored.
- Create evaluation mechanisms that have preset review waypoints, so that the organization can determine whether established goals are being met at, say, 6 months, 9 months, or a year.
- Incorporate feedback systems into the day-to-day activities of the organization.
- Incorporate feedback as part of a help desk system.
- Use office automation as a facilitator of the ICT strategy.
- Reevaluate the evaluation precepts regularly.

Clearly, the issues highlighted here affect all facets of the organization. It is imperative, then, that the superintendent and the CIO work as a team to address each of these issues. The superintendent needs to have enough understanding of technology to grasp in general terms how technology can be harnessed to accomplish the goals of the organization. Conversely, the CIO needs to be well-grounded in understanding the myriad issues and constituencies the superintendent deals with on a day-to-day basis. Both need to trust one another and work well together so that, along with other school leaders, they can conceive, plan, and implement the strategic initiatives of the organization.

CHAPTER EIGHT

SOME PITFALLS IN THE USE OF DATA—AND HOW TO AVOID THEM

ROY FORBES

T he intent of this chapter is to describe pitfalls associated with the use of data and to suggest some ways of avoiding them. I'm presenting this information in an informal manner. My intent is to try to make a complex topic understandable, and maybe even fun.

Data is your friend. It exists to assist you in making decisions. But approach it carefully! If not, it may turn around and bite you.

The six most important things to remember in approaching data are these:

1. Trust your intuition and experience.

2. Don't be afraid to ask questions.

3. Demand explanations in lay terms.

4. Ask about the limitations of the study, measurement instruments, and procedures used in collecting and analyzing the data.

5. Keep asking questions until you understand what is being presented.

6. Finally, ask yourself, "Does this make sense?"

Only when you have satisfactory, comprehensible answers to your questions should you make use of the data.

Data is your friend. It exists to assist you in making decisions. But approach it carefully! If not, it may turn around and bite you.

As is true of most things, there is a flip side to the above approach: It can be used to rationalize inaction. Sometimes, if you don't want to hear what the data are telling you, you may look for ways to discount the data instead of trying to understand the "friendliness" of the data. Hence, if not used objectively, some of the above approaches can be used to formulate excuses for not paying attention to the data and not using them in your decision-making processes.

Perhaps I need to say just a bit more about those six points, but if you feel as if you've got it, skip to the last paragraph prior to the next titled section of the chapter.

1. Trust Your Intuition and Experience. When you read a data-driven report, always ask yourself if the results or conclusions are what you would expect. If the findings don't line up with your expectations or experience, then it is time to take a deeper look. Your intuition could prove to be wrong, but how often does that happen to you?

2. Don't Be Afraid to Ask Questions. I grew up in the Old South, where politeness was (and, for some, continues to be) an important characteristic in how one conducts herself or himself. Directly questioning the statements of another was considered to be impolite. This cultural limitation can be a serious problem when it comes to the use of data. If you have questions, Southerner or not, don't hesitate to ask.

3. Demand Explanations in Lay Terms. Some researchers and evaluators only know how to write for their colleagues' consumption; hence, when they write reports, they feel compelled to use academic terms using the rationale that "only these terms" can specifically describe the data. Nonsense! All data reports can be put in terms that the general public can understand. If you do not have direct access to the author, then you need someone on your staff who can do the "translation."

4. *Ask About the Limitations of the Study, Measurement Instruments, and Procedures Used in Collecting and Analyzing the Data.* Assume that there is no such thing as a perfect study, instrument, data collection, or analysis procedure and you will most likely be on safe ground. Presume there are limits. Ask about those limitations. The limitations should be used as part of your decision-making process.

5. *Keep Asking Questions Until You Understand What Is Being Presented.* There is no need to add to this one. You get the picture.

6. *Finally, Ask Yourself, "Does This Make Sense?"* This takes us back to step 1. After making sure that you understand the data report and have a handle on all of the limitations, it is time to return to your intuition and experience, but with an openness and willingness to learn. With all of that in place, ask yourself if what you are reading or hearing makes sense. If your answer is yes, you are ready to decide whether you are going to use the data and, if so, how.

Now it's time to turn to some specific pitfalls that you should try to avoid. Each pitfall is explained in nonacademic terms and, with one exception, includes an actual example of the pitfall in action.

DON'T AUTOMATICALLY TRUST THE REPORT OR DOCUMENTATION

Let me start with a "war story" that illustrates my caution that you should not automatically trust reports and documentation. At one point during my career, I worked as a program analyst for one of the major defense contractors. The project on which I was working pertained to the development of a missile defense system for a naval fleet. The concept included a defensive missile and a guidance system. The system could, theoretically, detect enemy missiles that had been fired and posed a threat to the fleet. The system was designed to direct the launching of an interceptor missile whose purpose was to destroy the incoming enemy missile before it could cause any danger to the fleet.

My assignment was to develop an algorithm that would control a timing device on the missile. The purpose of the algorithm was to control when the missile was receiving a guidance signal from the system, when it was detecting a signal being bounced off the incoming enemy missile, and when the missile was sending information about the bounced signal back to the guidance system. All three of these stages were measured in nanoseconds.

Computers were in their prehistoric days at the time. Multitasking was an unknown concept, and computer operators only communicated with programmers through work orders. I developed the algorithm and set out to develop a simulation to test the mathematics. The process required that I write a simulation program and submit it to the computer lab for processing. If you made any mistakes in programming, you had to wait for the program to run and the printout to be returned with mistakes indicated. This was a repetitive, usually time-consuming process. I worked hard on the program, trying not to make any typos or other "idiot" mistakes. I remember programming the printing of "BOOM!!!" when the friendly missile had intercepted and successfully destroyed the enemy missile. I sent the program to the computer lab and had to wait until the next day to receive the results of my initial submission. I fully expected a thin printout listing programming errors. Instead, much to my surprise and pleasure, I received a 5-inch thick printout. I knew the program must have run on my very first attempt, so I quickly flipped to the back of the printout until I found the word *BOOM!!!* This meant that not only had the programming been correct, but that the algorithm was also correct.

After celebrating my joy with my colleagues, I started reviewing all the data. The deeper I delved into the printout, the more worried I became. (At this point, I must share the crucial fact that the missile had a nuclear warhead.) As I approached the page with the BOOM!!!, it became clear what had happened. The friendly missile had destroyed the enemy missile *seven nautical yards* above the deck of the ship that it was designed to defend. Obviously, this was not the success that I had just finished celebrating.

This imprinted for me another danger in using data: *Do not jump to conclusions.* The use of data requires a careful review of both the data and the processes used in collecting and analyzing the data. The

BOOM!!! may have been valid, but the implication was disastrous. Side note: In case you were wondering, the algorithm was correct. It was a programming error.

VALIDITY AND RELIABILITY: THE TERMS DON'T MATTER, BUT THE CONCEPTS ARE IMPORTANT

The jargon of statistics and data is full of complex and frightening-sounding terms. Two such terms are *validity* and *reliability*. When these terms were discussed in your statistics class, the instructor probably introduced the concepts using a couple of examples and then quickly moved to the methodology of establishing validity and reliability, using a complex statistical formula—hence losing most of the class except for the few "statistic-oriented" heads. Your concept of these two important features of data may therefore not have been adequately developed.

If you feel comfortable with your working knowledge of these important terms, then you may decide to skip to the next section. If you are not comfortable with the terms, or if you wish to reinforce your comfort level, then the following may be helpful. Having a sound working knowledge of these two concepts is extremely important for all who plan to use data in decision making.

I remember quite well when the concept of data validity became clear to me. I had studied the concept in class and thought I had a fairly good grasp of what it meant, but it took a real-life experience to bring the concept into sharp focus. Many years ago, while I was working in Louisville, Kentucky (and prior to the integration of the city and county school districts there), the following events occurred. The city school district, experiencing problems with vandalism, developed a plan to respond to this challenge. The focus of the plan was on the development of school and community spirit, including activities designed to make the facilities more attractive and to increase feelings of pride and ownership. The plan also included an evaluation component, so that the superintendent could learn if the plan was working.

Several of us worked on the evaluation plan. We decided that, since most of the vandalism involved glass breakage, we would limit our data collection to compiling information about how frequently glass was being replaced in the schools. Data were diligently compiled over a

6-month period. The data, when analyzed, showed a beautiful downward curve. Obviously, the plan for reducing vandalism was working!

A report for the Board of Education and a press release were prepared, and the results were released with much fanfare. Early the next day, the associate superintendent for school maintenance stopped by my office, carrying a copy of the local newspaper. He threw it on my desk and asked what this was all about. I tried to explain, but he interrupted, saying, "Don't you guys know that we have been replacing glass panels with plexiglass? That's the reason for the decline in the amount of glass being replaced."

> We sometimes conduct measurements, collect data, analyze data, and make decisions without having valid information.

We were not measuring what we thought we were measuring. Our data had no validity.

Although my example may be dated (Who uses the term *plexiglass* anymore?), the point is sound. We sometimes conduct measurements, collect data, analyze data, and make decisions without having valid information.

Probably one of the best examples today is the approach that is often taken in determining the effectiveness of professional development activities. When professional development activities are planned and implemented, the evaluation design often contains two components. First, teachers and others on the receiving end of the professional development are surveyed to determine their views on the usefulness of the activities. The second component is to compile and analyze results of student achievement tests. We analyze the "usefulness" and the "achievement" data and then reach conclusions about the effectiveness of the professional development.

This approach omits a crucial component: Were the teachers making classroom use of the knowledge and skills received during their involvement in the professional development activities? Without this information, there is no way of linking the data on usefulness and achievement. Without this link, we can make comparisons between the two sets of data, but we cannot establish causal relationships. Each of the two individual measures may be valid, but the *combination* may not be valid. If we want to make valid measures of professional development in terms of student performance, teacher observation data must be included. There is no shortcut.

Reliability also has its pitfalls. Recently, I have been involved in measuring the effectiveness of a series of Saturday camps for students in Grades K–2, 3–5, and 6–8. The purpose of these camps is to provide students with positive experiences related to learning science. One of the components of the evaluation is the observations of students to determine how engaged they are during the camp experiences. Observations are taken every 5 minutes. We found that engagement varies according to some easily identifiable factors: personality of the instructor, the way the group is organized, and the excitement or "fun-ness" of learning activities.

How do we know that our engagement observation is reliable? That is, how do we know that if someone else had been doing the observations, he or she would have recorded the same data? We did two things to establish reliability in our measures. First, we trained all of the observers. During the training, we instructed all of the observers to observe the same activities, and then we compared results and discussed the minor differences. Next, during the actual observations, we had one person assigned to each of the three groups, as well as a fourth person who floated among the groups. The observations of persons assigned to specific groups were compared with the observations of the floater. These two approaches allowed us to determine that we had a high level of agreement among the observers—hence, our data were reliable. Using the jargon, you would say that we had *high levels of inter-rater reliability.*

Conducting observations and not considering inter-rater reliability provides questionable data, and hence questionable evaluation results. Data reliability is important.

A mistake often made related to reliability is the use of a non-standardized approach to data collection. For example, one way of measuring the acquisition of knowledge during professional development activities is the use of pre- and post-concept mapping. To explain: Teachers involved in professional development designed to help with the implementation of a revised performance, standards-based mathematics curriculum may be asked to participate in pre- and post-concept mapping activities during each professional development session. At the beginning of the session, they are asked to list what they know about the concepts that will be presented during the session. At the end of the session, they are asked to list what they have learned.

If one instructor walks around the room during the pre- or post-mapping activities, encouraging the teachers to remember specific data by asking probing questions or by reminding them of a topic that was covered, the resulting data may be very different from those collected by another instructor who only provided directions. Although the same form may be used, the results may be quite different. Hence the data are not reliable. One way to avoid this type of reliability issue is to have an external evaluator present during the pre- and post-concept mapping activities, with a focus on determining if administration standards were being maintained.

TOO MUCH CONFIDENCE IN YOUR DATA

Once, while I was managing a relatively large operation that was almost totally dependent on federal funds, I detected a distinct probability that the budget would be cut by a sizable percentage. There were rumors that Congress was going to reduce the appropriation for the program by 20 percent, and we were already in the first quarter of the year that would have been affected by the reduction. I immediately put my data-collection skills into high gear, tapping the most reliable resources.

I had a one-person-removed direct link to the chairman of the Senate Appropriations Committee, who would be greatly influencing the decision related to the budget reduction. I was assured that there would indeed be a reduction, and that it most likely would be 20 percent. Therefore, I immediately started taking steps to prepare for the reduction. My first action was to inform staff members of the situation and to outline the steps necessary to prepare for the reduction. Our organization had multiple offices throughout a six-state region. I spoke directly to staff in one office and via a telephone conference call to staff in all the other offices. After providing information about our challenge and explaining the steps being taken to respond, I made an off-the-cuff remark that, if the budget reduction did not occur, I would dress up in a Chicken Little costume and run around saying that the sky was falling.

Fast forward to the next meeting, at which all staff members were present. There I was—dressed in my Chicken Little costume, running into the meeting yelling, "The sky is falling! The sky is falling!" I had put too much confidence in my data.

The flip side to placing too much confidence in your data—placing too little confidence in your data—is also a pitfall. There are statistical measures that can assist you in determining how much confidence to place in *quantitative* data. It is the *qualitative* information with which you must deal that's the tricky part. This is a real art form, and experience is your best ally. In addition, because all quanti-

The flip side to placing too much confidence in your data—placing too little confidence in your data—is also a pitfall.

tative data exist in a qualitative context, your best approach is to understand and appreciate the pitfalls to avoid in using data. I trust that the examples given in this section will assist you in developing such an understanding. The appreciation part is totally up to you.

DATA CONFIDENTIALITY: SOMETHING NOT TO BE IGNORED

This is a pitfall you *must* avoid. Data confidentiality is extremely important. The basic rules are rather simple:

- Hire a lawyer.
- Develop a policy pertaining to data confidentiality.
- Develop a set of procedures to be followed for implementing the policy.
- Implement the procedures.
- Monitor the implementation of the procedures.
- Use a zero-tolerance approach in dealing with infractions related to the release of data.
- Use a "three strikes, you're out" approach in dealing with infractions relating to other confidentiality procedures.

If you start to work in a new organization, most likely the data confidentiality policies and procedures are already in place. You can then start following the above rules at the implementation level. If you are the chief operating officer, however, then I suggest that you hire a lawyer, review the policies and procedures, make necessary changes, and then follow the remaining rules starting with the implementation of the procedures.

I do not believe that an example is necessary for this one. Avoiding the other pitfalls discussed in this chapter can save you trouble (and perhaps your job), but avoiding this pitfall can protect your personal freedom and financial security.

UNTAPPED DATA SOURCES

Don't always wait for the data to come to you. This will limit the information available for your process of decision making. You need to think of yourself as an explorer. Where do the necessary data exist that will help you to make better decisions? Once you have identified a potential source, then you will need to plan your exploration. Sometimes your explorations will take you into unfriendly territory, but like most explorers, you can generally find a way to accomplish your goal.

An example of an accomplished data explorer may help at this point. This example will probably strike closer to home with decision makers who are more involved with securing most of their operational funds than it will with those who are on the receiving end of state decisions for most of their funds. However, it's still a good example of exploring for data.

A school system in Oregon was dependent on tax funds related to the number of trees that were harvested in its district each year. This source of funds had been used for decades; little thought had been given to its continuation as a reliable source. Trees had always been harvested. Logging was an integral part of the culture. One sure way of becoming unpopular with this community was to do anything that made it appear that you were supporting environmentalists who expressed concerns about the clear-cutting of trees.

By now you may already know where this story is going, but it's worth telling. One brave local researcher and evaluator, a person who spent considerable time involved in outdoor activities, connected the dots between the system's future finances and a growing concern about the disappearance of pristine forests. He decided that he would project, given the current level of harvesting, when the forest acreage within the district would be cleared. Based on historical data from other areas that had been overlogged, he made some assumptions about how the level of logging would decrease over time as the number of forested areas declined. He then plotted the impact on the district's tax revenue. It was not an optimistic picture. It was a train wreck ready to happen, but breaking the news to the folks riding the train was an intensely touchy political issue. However, avoiding the issue would have been irresponsible. (This points to yet another pitfall, which I'll explore later under "Don't Be a Data Ostrich.")

My point is that the data pertaining to the impact on revenue were not something that would have been automatically generated. It required an unsolicited exploration. Who can say if the same would have happened if the local researcher had not had a strong connection with the outdoors? Possibly it could have come from an environmentalist seeking to bolster his or her position, but for the individual to have connected the dots between school district revenue and the cutting of trees would have been truly remarkable. It took a *data explorer* to find an important set of data—data that would have provided the district with time to plan for a dramatic change in the source of local revenue required to support its historically effective education of the community's youth.

You may not consider yourself to be a data explorer, but it is a skill that can be learned. I will leave that subject to someone writing about professional development and data-based decision making. However, locating untapped data resources is an important activity that should not be left to chance. At least twice a year, an activity specifically designed to identify untapped data sources should be undertaken by you and some of your colleagues.

DON'T BE A DATA NAZI

Another heading for this section could be, "With No Buy-In, It Won't Work."

Let's say you're a great user of data. You see the value of using data in decision making, and you want everyone to share your insight. Or you may have heard that data-driven decision making is the latest craze; since you want your school to be recognized as being on the cutting edge, you decide that data is the way to go. To bring everyone on board, however, requires a well-thought-out strategy. It doesn't happen simply by decreeing that it will be so.

Once, I visited a school where every hallway was full of data charts.

Requiring someone to use data does not work. Potential users must develop an appreciation for, and see the value in, using data in their decision-making processes.

Just about everything you could think of was on a chart someplace in that school. A small staff of people was dedicated to generating the charts. The process and the data were truly impressive. But, while interviewing teachers, it became clear that the data were not really being used in making decisions related to improving student performance. The teachers viewed the generation of data as just another chore that had been added to their already busy schedules. The principal had created the process and put it in place, but there was no buy-in by the teachers. Needless to say, student performance remained at the same levels that existed prior to the "data wallpaper."

Requiring someone to use data does not work. Potential users must develop an appreciation for, and see the value in, using data in their decision-making processes. Almost everyone uses data to make decisions. It is not that some people are anti-data. The problem is that they need help and guidance in increasing the ways in which they can use data to make better instructional decisions. If you are an effective leader, you already have skills related to developing buy-in. You just need to use your buy-in skills to move your school toward an environment where the use of data is valued, appreciated—and a reality.

Don't Kill the Messenger

Occasionally, you may receive information that you wish you had not received. The unwelcome information may take the form of low student test scores, questionable personnel review data, or projections about future revenue. It is unwise to blame the person who provides the information or to let this person be on the receiving end of actions in which you allow your frustrations to be the driving force.

I once had the misfortune to inherit a bad situation in which a competitive grant process had gone wrong. I set out to try and put in place procedures to make sure that the mistakes were not repeated. In the process, our team discovered a situation where it was obvious that colleagues had been involved in some questionable activities. We shared the information with the legal folks. The reaction toward the people involved in the questionable activities was swift, but it was what followed that affected our team. Although all of the questionable activities had happened prior to the formation of our team, some people in positions of authority had difficulty in separating the past from the present. When it became clear that our team was not respected and the team's competence was being unfairly questioned, I decided to depart, though I continued to respond to questions from the auditors investigating the questionable activities. It was not long before the other team members' services were terminated. Although one of the persons making decisions claimed to be well-read in management theory, I wonder if she had ever read any literature about not "killing the messenger" who bears the bad news.

This caution appears to be a "no-brainer" to me, but apparently it needs to be repeated: Be careful not to take any actions toward the deliverer of the information when your displeasure is with the data and not with the messenger.

DON'T LET YOUR EGO BE A BARRIER TO USING DATA

A good friend of mine was responsible for research and evaluation at a large membership organization. The organization began to experience a decline in membership, so he undertook a study to determine what was happening and to identify strategies to reverse the decline. His study revealed that the traditional sources of new members had been adversely affected by some of the organization's decisions. He projected that, given the current situation, the membership would continue to decline and that this would threaten the organization's survival. He identified some strategies that could be put in place to expand the potential membership pool. Then he packaged the information and submitted it to the Board of Directors for consideration.

His report was not well-received. The board's response was to disregard both the findings and the recommendations. Management "knew" that what they had been doing was the best way to run the organization and that things would be just fine. Their egos would not allow them to seriously consider findings that suggested that they had not been successfully managing the organization. Today, the organization is a glimmer of what it once was.

The lesson is this: Don't let your ego prevent you from considering *all* data and information. Organizations can always be improved upon; this is especially true for organizations facing challenges. The first step is to recognize that you have a challenge. The second step is to determine the seriousness of the challenge.

And third, plan your response accordingly. Data can be your friend as you walk through each step. The trick is not to let your ego be a factor.

Don't Be a Data Ostrich

Some people use the denial approach when it comes to dealing with data. Their lives are so busy that it's easy for them to set data aside. Other matters are calling for their attention. The data are placed somewhere on a lengthy to-do list, but are never given priority in a busy schedule.

Data have something to say, and it is important to listen. Unlike the person whose ego will not allow him or her to "hear" the data, the data ostrich hears, but through avoidance behavior the voice is muted.

Data have something to say, and it is important to listen. Unlike the person whose ego will not allow him or her to "hear" the data, the data ostrich hears, but through avoidance behavior the voice is muted.

Everyone may have a little ostrich in them. My own personal ostrich is usually associated with data-based information that pertains to an individual's performance. A couple of times, I have been badly burned by not "listening" to the data about an individual. Once, I put together a team of folks to represent the organization in the orals associated with a contract competition. I let the roles the people played in the organization determine their involvement in the process. I avoided considering other information, such as the ability to control nervous laugher and the ability to take questions seriously and not be flippant. The result was not good.

While evaluating programs, I often saw school leaders totally ignoring quantitative data pertaining to student performance and qualitative data pertaining to teacher morale. They appeared to be awfully busy. I can only assume that they considered the challenges to be insurmountable and had chosen to avoid what the data were saying about their school. They were not leaders. They limited themselves to being school administrators.

Avoid being an ostrich. Listen to and use the data.

FINALLY, DON'T MAKE DECISIONS
BASED ON INSUFFICIENT DATA

A little bit of data can be dangerous. You should not make decisions based on limited data. Sometimes that may be necessary because the data do not exist, but if additional sources of data are available, wait until you have a chance to review them before you make a decision.

While serving as the director of the National Assessment of Educational Progress (NAEP) from 1975–1982, I received a letter from a graduate student who was attending a rather well-known university. He requested that I send him the National Assessment because he wanted to replicate it for his dissertation.

Even at that time, the budget for the NAEP was approximately $3 million, with a sizable proportion of that sum allotted to data collection. We also had published procedures pertaining to the release of data. The student obviously had not done his homework before deciding on a dissertation topic. Economically, his decision was not feasible unless he was independently wealthy. With a little research, he would have known that his request was not congruent with NAEP item-release policies. He had based his decision on insufficient data.

IN CONCLUSION

My intent has been to informally provide you with some information about pitfalls that you may encounter as you use data in decision making. I trust that none of the pitfalls lessens your desire to use data. Remember, data can be one of your best friends. Decisions that are data-based can place you in a much stronger position than decisions that are only based on desires or political expediencies.

INDEX

CORWIN
PRESS

The Corwin logo—a raven striding across an open book—represents the union of courage and learning. Corwin is committed to improving education for all learners by publishing books and other professional development resources for those serving the field of PreK–12 education. By providing practical, hands-on materials, Corwin continues to carry out the promise of its motto: **"Helping Educators Do Their Work Better."**

The HOPE Foundation logo stands for Harnessing Optimism and Potential Through Education. The HOPE Foundation helps to develop and support educational leaders over time at district- and state-wide levels to create school cultures that sustain all students' achievement, especially low-performing students.

American Association
of School Administrators

The American Association of School Administrators, founded in 1865, is the professional organization for more than 13,000 educational leaders across the United States. AASA's mission is to support and develop effective school system leaders who are dedicated to the highest quality public education for all children. For more information, visit www.aasa.org.